THE NARRATIVE AGE

HOW LEADERS CAN INSPIRE CHANGE IN A POLARIZED WORLD

ISBN 978-3-9826237-2-6

Second printing, May 2024

Book design by Alyson von Massow RGD
Art Direction by Janet Levrel

THE NARRATIVE AGE

HOW LEADERS CAN INSPIRE CHANGE IN A POLARIZED WORLD

FRANK WOLF

CONTENTS

FOREWORD

BY MARTIN BÖHRINGER, COFOUNDER AND CEO, STAFFBASE

When Twitter launched in 2006, it instantly captivated me. It was so simple, just 140 characters and yet it changed the rules of news and communication, giving everyone access to the world's pulse in real time. I didn't just become a user; I was so enthusiastic that I spent more than three years driving research in that community, dedicating both my master's thesis and my Ph.D. to it. For me, Twitter marked the start of a new era for society, where equal access to information and fair discussion of opinions would be the norm. For a time it felt like an open, friendly place.

Fast forward to today. It turned out that Twitter indeed marked the start of the next phase for society, but not entirely as we had hoped. It is still the real-time center of the world if you want to keep up with what's happening in the moment, but polarization grows, and instead of encouraging curiosity about differing opinions, we observe people shouting at each other. I'm sure you know what I mean and have likely experienced it yourself. If you're on social media, you have to think twice about what you post and why. It has turned into a contentious arena.

So, what has changed since 2006? Unfortunately, social media did not turn the world into a place of common understanding as we had dreamed. Rather, the online world is made up of countless echo chambers. As humans, we have a deep desire to belong to like-minded groups, which reinforce our opinions and beliefs. We will go to great lengths to filter information and we favor messages that confirm our view of the world. This confirmation bias, the tendency to search for, interpret, and recall information in a way that confirms our preexisting beliefs, is what opens the door to echo chambers. And once we are safely inside our like-minded chamber, another effect begins to kick in: group polarization. When people who think alike come together, their discussions often push them to agree with opinions that are even stronger than the ones they started with. This phenomenon isn't new and has in fact been well researched for many years now. For instance, a study in 1973 assessed whether federal district court judges behaved differently when they sat alone compared to sitting in small groups. The results were pretty astonishing. Judges who sat alone while deliberating took extreme action 35 percent of the time, whereas judges who sat in a group of three took extreme action 65 percent of the time. Even trained, professional decision-makers are subject to the influences of group polarization.[1]

Groups aren't bad. In fact, they are necessary for societal health and individual wellbeing. At our core, we need to belong and feel valued. But those desires can sometimes have unintended negative consequences. In an effort to gain approval and belonging, members may shift their own opinions to align more closely with, or even push the boundaries of, what they perceive to be the dominant viewpoint. On social media, people may share amplified versions of their actual opinions coming from "the loudest voices" in order to attract attention and signal affiliation.[2] In an effort to feel valued or validated, members of a like-minded group will also gather arguments that confirm their own beliefs, ignoring or avoiding those that may point in a different direction.

Initially, Twitter was based on principles that would challenge the mechanisms of group polarization. Your timeline only consisted of postings from the people you followed, including retweets, which was the main method the platform used to continually get fresh ideas in front of you. A broad choice of who you followed rewarded you with serendipity — the happy surprise of finding a new idea when you weren't specifically looking for it.[3]

However, X, Facebook, Instagram, TikTok, and most other social media platforms have learned that there is another way to assemble your feed which is more engaging and lucrative than the "follower content only" model. It's built "just for you" with the help of Artificial Intelligence (AI) and is optimized to drive maximum advertising revenue by extending usage, aka scroll time. Your highly personalized timeline is designed to keep you engaged for as long as possible. And guess what we love to engage with the most? Content that confirms our view of the world. The algorithm prioritizes presenting our own views to us from the loudest voices, because they spark maximum engagement. This might feel good on an individual level, but as a society, we pay a high price for it: we live in a polarized world where we no longer seem able to agree even on basic facts.

There are situations where differing opinions cannot be avoided. Family comes to mind. Do you dread going to family events because of controversial discussions? You're not alone. 75 percent of people don't want to talk about politics at Thanksgiving,[4] and politically diverse Thanksgivings are half an hour shorter than politically uniform ones.[5] The same applies to the workplace, where you generally cannot choose your colleagues. Only 20 percent of people would be willing to work alongside someone who strongly disagrees with them or their point of view.[6]

So here we are, choosing echo chambers as our key source of information. If forced to interact with people of opposing opinions, we try to avoid discussions, withdraw from the situation, or engage without empathy.

But humanity simply cannot afford to entrench itself in our cozy confirmation bias. We have urgent problems to solve, and we need to work together to make that happen. The Club of Rome is an organization of scientists that addresses global challenges through research. It first raised the issue of a looming climate crisis in 1972, and 50 years later, it published the book *Earth for All: A Survival Guide for Humanity.* The authors write, "The most significant challenge of our day is not climate change, biodiversity loss, or pandemics. The most significant problem is our collective inability to distinguish between fact and fiction."[7] Most problems we face are complex, and what's needed is the empathy, patience, and expertise to understand the facts and create a solution. Polarization pushes oversimplified answers that might be great for getting attention on social media — but it will not help solve our challenges.

How can we band together again?

For ten years, we've witnessed people who have the ability to overcome these barriers. Staffbase, the employee communication company that Frank Wolf and I cofounded in 2014, has worked with a great number of corporate communication teams and leaders who possess a unique skill: they can bring people together toward common objectives. Despite individual differences that seem to block us in so many aspects of everyday life, these communicators manage to inspire people toward collective goals, focusing on what connects people rather than what pulls them apart.

As a business, Staffbase aims to help organizations bring people together to achieve great things. To do this, we are building the first end-to-end communications platform for organizations and are creating a community for communicators and leaders to learn, share best practices, and stay on the cutting edge of the field. So far, we have been focused on equipping leaders and communicators to get their message to their audience in the right place and at the right time.

But there is another key component to inspirational communication: understanding *why* stories resonate with an audience. How do you create openness to new perspectives and align people behind common goals? A shift is needed away from focusing solely on the messages we send and the stories we tell. Today, we need to understand what happens in the mind of the audience receiving those messages. This is where we enter the fascinating world of narratives, a superpower that successful communicators understand and utilize in their work. Story and narrative are often used interchangeably, but they are distinct concepts, and whoever understands the difference will discover a world of powerful insights. Narratives are often hidden in plain sight, and precisely because of this, have a huge impact on how we perceive ourselves, the organizations we interact with, and the society in which we live.

This book reveals the secrets of some of the most successful organizations and movements in the world — from SpaceX to DeBeers to the *Barbie* movie — explaining how they have masterfully utilized the power of narratives to inspire their audiences. Frank has spent more than a year researching the latest scientific insights, diving deep into real-life examples, and learning about the best practical ways to bring narratives to life. A trained marketer, Frank has championed the communications field throughout his career, with more than 20 years of consulting experience in the industry, tenure as Staffbase's Chief Marketing Officer, and as a contributor to the Forbes Communications Council and other thought leadership institutes.

The topic of narratives has already been explored in quite a few cases. And yet, leaders and communicators are still far from fully capitalizing on the insights and using them to create change. Moreover, most of the research has so far been discussed in siloed communities or buried in academic papers, making it difficult to access and hard to digest. The goal of this book is to make knowledge about narratives easily accessible and understandable. Through a mix of research insights alongside countless practical examples, it will show you how to apply narrative management in your everyday work.

INTRODUCTION
THE VALLEY OF THE CLUELESS

When the Berlin Wall fell in 1989, I had spent the first 14 years of my life in a city in East Germany named Dresden. In fact, Dresden is still my home today. The city is situated in a beautiful valley alongside the Elbe River. During East German times, its geographical position led to a unique quirk: it was notoriously difficult to catch West German TV and radio signals here. This peculiar situation earned our city the nickname "The Valley of the Clueless."

Unlike most other people in East Germany, we were completely cut off from Western media. All we had were government-controlled channels, where news strictly adhered to the narrative of socialist propaganda. But occasionally, I had the opportunity to glimpse outside the socialist world. My grandparents lived in a small village where they could receive West German television. For us children, the highlight of a visit was turning on the big TV and diving into a world that felt drastically different from the forced limitations of our own. Shows like *The Fall Guy* and *Knight Rider* captivated me as a boy, but we would also watch commercials for shampoo or dish soap with equal fascination.

Even without these regular peeks into the West, we knew not to take our own media's stories at face value. In a dictatorship, you only hear good things about your country. On the evening news, it was reported how companies and workers had successfully met or exceeded the government's plans and how the produced goods would raise the population's standard of living. Negative reports were always about the failings of capitalist countries, where unemployment and drug use seemed to run rampant.

The problem with these news reports was that they failed to match our reality. The basic supply of food was stable, but beyond that, almost everything else was scarce. If your heating broke down, good luck finding a technician and spare parts. Looking for fashionable clothing or attractive furniture? You might as well make it yourself. Scarcity was everywhere, from simple items like fruits and vegetables to technical consumer goods such as stereo systems. It was even difficult to find a liveable apartment. One of the most notorious examples of scarcity was the wait time for a new car — more than 15 years! And once you finally had a car, there weren't many places to visit since traveling to most other countries was forbidden. The apparent neglect of capitalist societies being touted on the news also didn't match the rich landscape we could see with our own eyes on Western television.

Yet while the regime's depiction of East Germany didn't match our reality, it was dangerous to question or express critical opinions openly. You would see stories in the official news about socialist leaders visiting factories, smiling, and shaking hands. But behind the facade, everyone knew that voicing concerns or pointing out contradictions could get you into trouble fast. I know people who found themselves imprisoned for years, just for telling a single regime-critical joke.

People in such a fearful environment become extremely adept at reading between the lines and joking in whispers while walking the tightrope of what's allowed and what is tacitly forbidden. From a perspective of power, this may have been enough to trick an onlooker into thinking that everyone in East Germany was well-aligned and that society was functional.

This part of my life taught me a lesson I will never forget: **Controlling the channels and the message doesn't guarantee the winning of hearts and minds.** People instinctively compare what they're being told to what they actually witness and experience. Any disconnect chips away at trust, one disappointment at a time. This principle holds true not only in dictatorships but also in any group setting — including businesses. It becomes increasingly challenging to maintain credibility when the gap is constantly widening between what leaders say and what people see on the ground.

After the Wall came down, we learned more about the delusional picture of reality that had been drawn by many of our former East German leaders. They had lost all connection to the things people really cared about. This stands in stark contrast to great leaders like Steve Jobs and many others who also seemed to challenge reality with their aspirational vision of the future. Such visionaries are able to connect their far-reaching ideas with people's present identity and the realities they face. This is the art and science of great communication, and it's deeply rooted in learning what your audience knows and believes. The desire to learn more about these mechanisms of effective communication has driven me for most of my life.

This passion inspired me to study marketing, took me into the field of communications, and ultimately led to the founding of Staffbase. I had previously worked on countless digital communication projects. While my work was able to reach desk-bound audiences, time and again it left out the frontline workers who lacked access to desktop PCs. Connecting deskless workers via a mobile app on their mobile devices became more than just another channel for many of our customers; it sparked a revolution in their organizational culture. For the first time, they could truly connect with their frontline workers at scale, hear their unfiltered feedback and ideas, and ensure their communication could change hearts and minds.

These experiences taught me that all great communicators share a common trait: they know that it's not enough to simply send a message or tell a story. Instead, they harness the ability to connect messages with the ultimate intention of moving hearts and minds. In other words, they've mastered the ability to understand existing narratives and even create new ones. Narratives inspire people, which is why the idea of writing this book gripped me from the start.

Solving problems in our polarized world hinges on recognizing and addressing the facts and the realities of the challenges we face. My goal with this book is to combine the current state of narrative research with practical examples and actionable ideas that will show you how to utilize the power of narratives in your work. As the world becomes more complex and volatile, it's important for those of us with good intentions to use effective, fact-based stories and narratives to unite and inspire our audiences. After all, we left the Valley of the Clueless long ago. And we did so by speaking up.

THINGS I HOPE YOU'LL LEARN IN THIS BOOK

The imagined world is important to the real world

Chapter 1 explores how the imagined world of narratives and stories has become fundamental to how we understand the real world. Reputation is vital for organizations to survive and thrive, and narratives are the way to actively shape reputation in an increasingly fast-changing and complex world.

Narratives and stories aren't the same

Chapter 2 delves deeply into the difference between narratives and stories, listing seven reasons why narratives are more powerful than individual stories. Understanding this distinction offers numerous insights for communication. For instance, creating resonance with your audience requires alignment with their personal narrative landscape.

Narrative maps are the key to understanding your audience

Chapter 3 explores the different types of narratives, such as master narratives and local narratives, that make up the narrative landscape. It will show you how to develop a narrative map for your communications strategy.

With all the narrative basics in place, Chapters 4, 5, and 6 show how you can apply these insights to the most common and impactful communication challenges.

Narratives are hard to change – but it can be done

Chapter 4 covers ways to change existing narratives, which starts with recognizing the parts of a narrative landscape that are in fact changeable. The fascinating part for me was learning that our initial instinct to counter existing beliefs might often not be the best strategy to agree upon a new point of view.

You can create inspiring vision and mission statements

If you want to build the future, you need to dream it first. This is the guiding theme for Chapter 5, our deep dive into North Star narratives. I have to admit that I never liked the concept of vision, mission, and purpose because it felt confusing and hard to grasp for our own company. A lot of customers I speak with also struggle with this concept. The approach laid out in Chapter 5 helped us at Staffbase to redefine our vision and mission in a much more impactful way.

Narratives protect reputation and build a competitive advantage

A vision for the future can only become a reality if the current business thrives and the company's reputation is built and protected. Chapter 6 introduces the term "narrative moat" to describe all key narratives, such as value and employer narratives, that an organization needs to nurture and grow. Both a narrative moat and the North Star narrative are highly impactful assets to every business, and leaders need to sufficiently protect and develop this competitive advantage

Bringing narratives to life is the focus of the final two chapters.

Communication campaigns need strategies and not just plans

Chapter 7 dissects the dynamics of how communications campaigns can create maximum impact by embracing both strategy and improvisation. It discusses the difference between a plan and a strategy and how a theory of change is a great tool for mapping out strategic communication.

The Narrative Age is here and it's time to get ready

Lastly, Chapter 8 discusses which skills, processes, and tools need to be in place for any organization to successfully manage its reputation and narratives to gain a competitive advantage in our ever-changing world.

A Final Note

A key insight of the book is that our view of the world is necessarily subjective. This also applies to my particular point of view. As much as I am trying to build the case about narratives from a point of neutrality, I am fully aware that my perspective is colored by my own personal history. Different people may view narratives in various ways, either positively or negatively, depending upon their subjective perspective. Alternative interpretations of the narratives I present in the book that differ from my own are to be expected and are, of course, entirely valid. However, the way in which narratives are constructed — whether they're "good" or "evil" — is more of an objective reality.

Solving problems in our polarized world hinges on recognizing and addressing the facts and the realities of the challenges we face. My goal with this book is to combine the current state of narrative research with practical examples and actionable ideas that will show you how to utilize the power of narratives in your work. As the world becomes more complex and volatile, it's important for those of us with good intentions to use effective, fact-based stories and narratives to unite and inspire our audiences instead of further dividing them. After all, we left the Valley of the Clueless long ago. And we did so by speaking up.

1. THE NARRATIVE AGE

BANK RUNS USED TO BE SLOW

The warning, a single sentence, arrived in David Murray's inbox on March 9, 2023: There's a bank run underway, and we recommend you withdraw your funds immediately. Murray, the cofounder of an employee performance management company in San Francisco, had millions of dollars sitting in his accounts at Silicon Valley Bank (SVB). With bank deposits in the USA only being insured up to $250,000, he risked losing significant capital and even going bankrupt if the message was true.[1]

A bank run is an urgent crisis. Many customers suddenly withdraw their money because they're afraid that the bank might fail. This fear can spread quickly, like a rumor, and cause even more people to try to take out their deposits. So, after verifying the email and seeing the steep drop in the stock price of the bank's parent company, SVB Financial, Murray and his colleagues hurried to withdraw the company's cash. There was no need to rush to the branch. They could just log into their online banking software and, within 30 minutes, move every dollar to another bank.

Panicked SVB clients withdrew $42 billion USD from the bank on Thursday, March 9 — equivalent to nearly $500,000 USD per second over a 24-hour period. Many more failed to get their money out. By Friday morning, SVB was insolvent and under government control.

At Staffbase, we experienced the situation firsthand. We were also an SVB customer, and the panicked emails from investors asking their portfolio companies to withdraw money also landed immediately in our inbox. Fortunately, we did not have deposits at SVB but had agreed on a credit line with them in case we wanted to invest more money into our expansion. This option was suddenly off the table for us, and we had to start from scratch with another bank.

The SVB bank run unfolded at an unprecedented pace — the fastest in history. In comparison, the biggest bank run of the 2007–2008 financial crash saw $16.7 billion USD withdrawn from Washington Mutual, a savings and lending bank, over the course of 10 days.

The speed of the collapse was fueled by more than just emails and fast withdrawals via online banking. "It was a bank sprint, not a bank run, and social media played a central role in that," said Michael Imerman, a professor at the Paul Merage School of Business at the University of California-Irvine.

On Thursday evening, word circulated on Twitter that billionaire venture capitalist Peter Thiel had advised his invested companies to close their accounts with Silicon Valley Bank. Later, OpenAI CEO Sam Altman tweeted: "the speed of the world has changed. things can unwind fast. people talk fast. people move money fast."[2]

At its core, a bank run is about a breakdown of trust. People trust that their money is safe in a bank and that they can access it whenever needed. This works because everybody shares the same belief, and as long as this communal belief persists, institutions like banks and corporations can exist. But what exactly are people putting their trust in? What is this communal belief based on?

THE SURVIVAL OF THE REAL WORLD DEPENDS ON THE IMAGINED WORLD

70,000 years ago, Homo sapiens developed a sudden and remarkable increase in cognitive capabilities, including the ability to create and use complex language. Unlike other animal communication systems, human language allows for the expression of abstract concepts like myths, beliefs, the past, and the future.

Yuval Noah Harari is an Israeli historian and a professor in the Department of History at the Hebrew University of Jerusalem. He gained international recognition for his book *Sapiens: A Brief History of Humankind*. According to Harari, the cognitive revolution kick-started a rapid cultural evolution. Humans began to create sophisticated tools, art, and companies, and eventually even landed on the moon. These advancements were only possible because of our capacity to collectively imagine things, which gives us the unprecedented ability to cooperate in large numbers. President John F. Kennedy spoke in 1962 about the ambition to land a man on the moon by 1969. While nothing real was created in that moment, something far more important happened: he stirred the collective imagination in millions of minds. This shared vision guided and enabled the collaboration of about 400,000 engineers, scientists, technicians, and administrative staff that made the Apollo Moon landings possible.

Harari uses the carmaker Peugeot as an example of a company that exists because humans collectively believe in its existence. On a tangible level, Peugeot is made up of various physical entities like factories, employees, and products. However, the "company" itself is an imagined reality. It is not an objective part of the natural world but rather a construct of human imagination, defined by legal and social agreements.

Indeed, as Harari notes, we are at a point where the imagined world is fundamental to the real world:

> Ever since the cognitive revolution, sapiens have thus been living in a dual reality. On the one hand the objective reality of rivers, trees and lions and on the other hand the imagined reality of gods, nations and corporations. As time went by, the imagined reality

> became ever more powerful, so that today the very survival of rivers, trees and lions depends on the grace of imagined entities such as the United States and Google.[3]

An organization like Silicon Valley Bank is a complex network of stories constructing an imagined reality, including the past, present, and future. Customers like startups chose SVB because they believed that it was the bank that best understood their needs. The value of SVB's stock hinged on the collective belief of its shareholders in its worth. Employees decided to work at SVB, driven by their conviction that the organization would persist and flourish in the future. And yet, SVB is an example of how quickly trust in any imagined entity can vanish.

Organizations need a moat to protect their belief systems and build a competitive advantage. In a business context, a moat is the term used to describe a company's competitive advantage that is difficult for competitors to imitate or overcome. It protects the business much like a moat protects a castle. Strong narratives are able to build long-lasting competitive advantages for organizations. At the same time, the term moat aligns very well with the idea of the reputational capital that needs to be built up before it's ever needed. The moat we are talking about here is called reputation.

REPUTATION – YOU CAN'T FAKE IT

> *Companies are actually engaged in mortal combat for the respect and trust of consumers, investors, employees, and the public at large. Respect and trust build reputation, and that's what creates a competitive advantage.*[4]

This is a quote from Charles Fombrun, one of the pioneers of managing and measuring reputation. What others think of a company — its reputation — can be measured and quantified in real numbers: SVB stock fell from $267 USD on March 8 to less than one dollar a couple of days later. Apple's brand is worth more than half a billion dollars.[5] Customers pay $2,000 USD for a leather bag from Louis Vuitton, which has an estimated production cost of less than $200 USD. The imagined value has become a critical part of corporate valuation and can even outweigh the tangible assets.

A good reputation has to be earned by reliable and responsible activities, services, or products. Reputation cannot be projected or faked in the long term; it has to be built from the inside. An organization cannot just "look good," it has to "be good." In addition, good deeds do not constitute a reputation if nobody knows about them. They have to be communicated.[6]

While reputation is built by being good and communicating about it, it's often the latter part that receives the most attention. Traditionally, communication focuses on external audiences and is much more visible. This means reputation management might be reduced to an outside-in approach, creating image campaigns with little to say about the actual identity of an organization.

Sustainable reputation management will only be possible with an authentic corporate identity. There is broad evidence in reputation research that external organizational image and internal organizational identity are deeply interlinked. As the founder of the modern practice of corporate public relationships Arthur W. Page said in one of his core principles: "Realize an enterprise's true character is expressed by its people." This means a good reputation is best built on the organization's true core identity.[7] Companies that are successful at reputation management think about it from the inside out, starting with employees.

Every company derives value from a positive perception by others. This reputational capital is intangible but impactful. A company with a large stock of reputational capital gains a competitive advantage against rivals because its reputation enables it to hire and keep the best talent, charge premium prices for its products, achieve lower marketing costs, or keep the trust of its stakeholders during a crisis.

When you trust someone, you give them the benefit of the doubt. If that person gets in trouble, you listen to their side of the story before jumping to conclusions. Companies need to build that same benefit of the doubt among their stakeholders. Without a strong reputation, companies risk not having a receptive audience for their story when they need one the most.

According to a study based on the attitudes of 20,000 consumers conducted by market research firm Ipsos, this willingness to give the benefit of the doubt is tightly linked to overall trust. Among people who trust a company a great deal, 51 percent say they would definitely give that company the benefit of the doubt in a crisis. Among people who feel neutral towards a company, that percentage shrinks to just 10 percent.

The study also shows that a good reputation impacts advertising and product use enormously. People who trust a company are more likely to see the ads in the first place, to find the ads memorable, and to believe the ads. Of those who "trust a great deal" in a company, 94 percent are likely to believe the ads they see, compared to 48 percent of those who "distrust a little" and 32 percent of those who "distrust a great deal."[8]

Research from the Annenberg Center for Public Relations at the University of Southern California found clear evidence that "consumers are making more demands, employees are more vocal and investors are scrutinizing every aspect of a company's behavior. Corporate reputation has become the determining factor for the products they buy, the jobs they choose, and the stocks they invest in." Consumers, employees, and investors all agree that reputation matters and it's influencing their decisions on what to buy, where to work, and where to invest.[9]

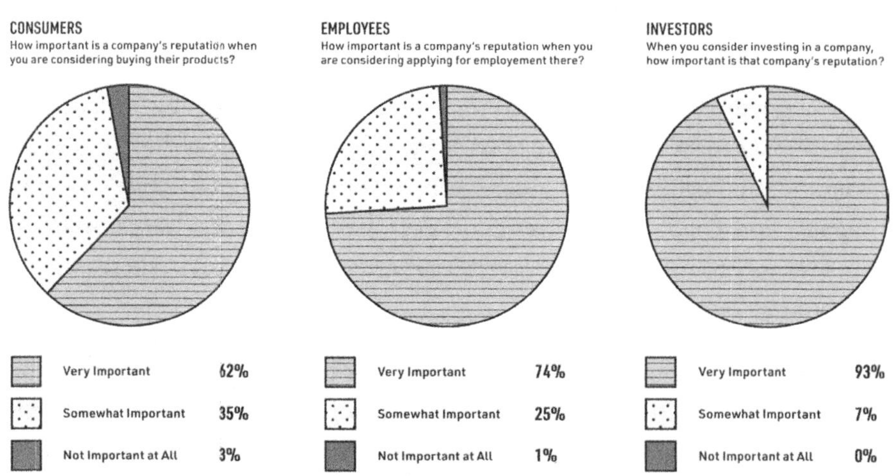

Consumers, employees, and investors overwhelmingly rate the importance of a company's reputation as very important or somewhat important for their decisions. Source: 2023 Global Communications Report. USC Annenberg Center for Public Relations.

Unfortunately, Silicon Valley Bank did not have strong enough reputational capital or communication to master their liquidity crisis. It was in a tough spot financially because of too much investment into long-term bonds, which temporarily lost value with rising interest rates. They also failed to convincingly explain their side of the story and made several communication errors.

The first miscalculation was to address a financial analyst audience with a standard press release without considering the side effects on their financially less knowledgeable but more sensitive customer audience. This means SVB shared their most critical news of the year without reassurance to their core customers — startup founders and venture capital firms. This is a very closely connected community where word travels fast. Startups are fragile organizations without many safety nets. For hundreds of startups with payroll runs coming up in days or weeks, SVB was holding all of their funds. It didn't help that this audience was always on high alert and, more often than not, in survival mode. They were ready to make fast, conclusive decisions.

The press release itself used technical language to announce the need to raise money: "SVB Financial Group Announces Proposed Offerings of Common Stock and Mandatory Convertible Preferred Stock." The press text did not explain the reasons for the raise or any reassurance about the strength of the business otherwise. After the press release, SVB stayed quiet and failed to react as worries rose in the community.

Almost a full day later, SVB's CEO Greg Becker made another communication misstep. On a Zoom call, he gathered key customers to reassure them about the bank's stability. He said, "My ask is to stay calm because that's what is important. We have been long-term supporters of you — the last thing we need you to do is panic."[10] Unfortunately, this message created the opposite effect to what was intended: social proof that everyone else thought this was a bank run. Getting funds out of SVB might be the only appropriate response.

Leaders often cannot control events, but they can control the context under which events are seen.[11] SVB released significant news that could trigger fear and confusion. The announcement came with minimal context, delayed outreach to customers and influencers, and messaging likely to incite panic, hinting at the possibility of a bank run.[12]

SVB did not have a communications professional on its leadership team, and no crisis communications plan was in place. This communication failure had various root causes, but it could only happen because the bank's leadership was not prepared to protect its reputation and keep the trust of its stakeholders during a crisis.

But this bank run was much more than a failure in external communication. Since reputation and trust are built from the inside out, the bank's risk management procedures were heavily criticized in the aftermath. In the first congressional hearing after the SVB bankruptcy, Michael Barr, the Fed's vice chairman for supervision, criticized SVB for going months without a chief risk officer and for how it modeled interest-rate risk, which he said *"was not at all aligned with reality."* Fed supervisors had flagged such issues with bank management, but they went unaddressed.[13] The bank failed to build reputational capital around its risk management, and based on the Fed's insights, this external lack of reputation was caused by an insufficient internal risk management culture.

FOUR CATALYSTS RAISE THE BAR FOR REPUTATION MANAGEMENT

The SVB crisis didn't happen in a vacuum. In fact, big shifts in reputation management paradigms were unfolding that made the speed and severity of the situation possible. For many decades, managing an organization's reputation was a relatively straightforward affair. Companies were primarily focused on generating profits for their shareholders, and this singular goal shaped their public image strategies. The perception of employees about their employer was not a significant factor in shaping external reputation, which often operated independently of the internal realities within the organization. This scenario was underpinned by a slower pace of change and a higher degree of predictability in business planning.

In this environment, the task of communication and public relations departments was to forge strong relationships with a handful of influential journalists and media gatekeepers, strategically feeding them the right stories to shape public perception. This approach was effective when the flow of information was more controlled and less instantaneous, allowing businesses to plan and execute their reputation management strategies in a stable and predictable environment.

Reputation management expert Charles Fombrun wrote in 1996: "Indeed, learning to actively manage reputational capital and the human and intellectual assets it encompasses may be the most crucial and strategic task that our executives face as they struggle to compete in today's increasingly competitive, information-rich business environment."[14]

He wrote these words nearly 30 years ago, already back then feeling that the information-rich environment was overwhelming executives. From today's perspective, things in 1996 were much slower and easier to navigate compared to now! The adoption of the internet occurred in the late 1990s, and social media began its ascent in the mid-2000s. Since then, a constant stream of technological innovations and societal changes has continued to challenge organizations in protecting and building their reputations. Specifically, there are four catalysts that substantially raise the bar for the reputation management of organizations. Let's take a closer look at what those are.

1. The ever-increasing pace of change

An impressive example of this comes from a business that for many years seemed impossible to attack and disrupt. Google, the world's largest search engine with a market share of more than 90 percent, was caught by surprise by the launch of OpenAI's groundbreaking AI service, ChatGPT. Google felt the pressure to respond and showcased its own AI solution called Bard in a live-streamed presentation a couple of months later. Bard was asked to provide information about the discoveries of the James Webb Space Telescope (JWST). Unfortunately, Bard delivered an incorrect answer, wrongly stating that the JWST was used to take the very first pictures of a planet outside our solar system. In reality, the first pictures of exoplanets were taken by the European Southern Observatory's Very Large Telescope in 2004.

While one could easily dismiss this as a minor mistake by an otherwise impressive piece of technology, Google has long been the epitome of a market-leading company, seemingly unable to be caught by competitors.

Now, it was suddenly chasing another leader in AI technology. Shares in Google's parent company Alphabet fell 7.7 percent after the presentation, wiping $100 billion USD off its market value.[15]

AI represents the latest in a continuous wave of change sweeping over organizations. Previous digital advancements, such as the internet and social media, have spawned countless new business models while rendering others obsolete. Extraordinary events like the COVID-19 pandemic and international conflicts like the war in Ukraine have altered business landscapes and operational conditions. The climate crisis necessitates a fundamental shift in how humanity produces, consumes, travels, eats, and even spends their leisure time. This process of change has only just begun and will need to persist for decades to achieve the zero-emission goals essential for humanity's survival. Change might seem rapid now, but it will only accelerate from this point forward.

Change poses a challenge in the real world, where physical reconstruction is necessary, but it's an even greater challenge in the world of imagined institutions. Organizations are constructed on countless stories held in the minds of their members and stakeholders. Adapting to change involves rewriting these narratives, discarding past best practices, and fostering new shared visions of the future. That's why managing change is a key challenge for those shaping and maintaining reputation.

Even though it has been a significant contributor to AI research, Google has struggled to effectively integrate these findings into its products. The resources and sense of urgency are in place, and Google now faces the challenge of delivering on two fronts: accelerating its efforts through its Gemini program to become a formidable contender in AI technology and rebuilding its reputation as the world's leading AI organization.

2. Shareholder value is no longer the sole focus

Nobel laureate economist Milton Friedman wrote in 1970: "There is one and only one social responsibility of business — to use its resources and engage in activities designed to increase its profits." Companies must obey the law. But beyond that, their job is to make money for shareholders.[16] For many years, this was the guiding principle of most large corporations worldwide.

Now, organizations are starting to change their minds in an atmosphere of widening economic inequality, climate change, and deepening distrust of business. In 2019, 181 CEOs of America's largest corporations — united in an organization called Business Roundtable — adopted a new statement on the purpose of corporations. They declared that companies should not only serve their shareholders but also deliver value to their customers, invest in employees, deal fairly with suppliers, and support the communities in which they operate. Profits remain the foundation that allows looking beyond shareholders, and the best way to generate these profits long-term is by actively managing and driving reputation with all stakeholders. Only then will a company have a "license to operate."[17]

One of the most famous and far reaching examples comes from the outdoor apparel maker Patagonia. Founder Yvon Chouinard has transferred his family's ownership of Patagonia, worth approximately $3 billion USD, to a specially created trust and a nonprofit organization. These entities were established to maintain the company's independence and guarantee that all its profits — around $100 million annually — are dedicated to fighting climate change and conserving undeveloped land worldwide.[18]

Think of a license to operate as a company's unwritten permission slip from society. It's not about legal rights but about earning trust and approval from everyone touched by the business. A major driver of this movement are employees. The Edelman Future of Corporate Communications Study 2023 asked chief communication officers: "Which stakeholders are putting the most pressure on your organizations to act on social issues?" Employees lead the field with 61 percent of responses naming them, followed at a considerable distance by investors and NGOs, each at 21 percent. Customers are even further behind, with just 7 percent.[19]

Note that this extends beyond matters directly related to a company's immediate business operations. CEOs are under increasing pressure to take a public stance on key societal challenges. A contributing factor to these heightened expectations is high levels of trust in companies and leaders. In an increasingly polarized environment, businesses are the most trusted institutions — more so than NGOs, the government, and the media. This role of integration is particularly significant as the majority of people in Western countries concur with the statement, "Our country is more divided today than in the past."[20]

In this environment, reputation can no longer be managed defensively. In the past, saying nothing and staying silent in the background was, in many cases, the obvious and best option for reputation management. Now, just like a brand, reputation must be positioned. Being ready to respond to these issues requires knowing your organization's values, planning for worst-case scenarios, and establishing processes to analyze and determine what you will or will not act upon, why, and in what manner.

3. The decentralized media landscape

In June 2020 star player Cristiano Ronaldo sat for a press conference at the UEFA Euro soccer tournament. Before answering questions, he removed two bottles of Coca-Cola placed in front of him and replaced them with a bottle of water. While doing so, he remarked, "Água!" (Portuguese for "water"), seemingly endorsing water over soda.[21]

Following Ronaldo's action, the market value of Coca-Cola dropped by $4 billion USD. Ronaldo has over 600 million followers on Instagram, while Coca Cola is at three million. When it comes to social media reach, one of the most well-known and most valuable brands in the world does not stand a chance against a high-profile athlete.

We all know that social media has dramatically changed how information is shared, amplified, and consumed. The most profound shift with social media is that it turns a traditional one-way publisher-to-audience model into a much more complex relationship. Audience members can become actors themselves, commenting, liking, and remixing images, information, and stories.

Though most consumers don't have the reach of Cristiano Ronaldo, we have more power than ever before. You can give your hotel ratings on booking.com or complain about the service in a restaurant on Tripadvisor. This is also increasingly relevant for B2B companies like Staffbase. Our customers are enterprises, and they can visit feedback portals like Gartner Peer Insights to discuss their experiences with implementing our platform. That's why one of the most important indicators for our business is how much value our platform actually delivers to our customers. Nearly 40 percent of consumers have come to distrust traditional advertising, but a majority will take online peer reviews as a much more reliable and authentic source of information before making a decision.[22]

Yet media usage habits are very personal, and many leaders and decision-makers fail to recognize how much has changed, especially for younger generations. I was born in 1975 and I use platforms like LinkedIn; X, formerly known as Twitter; and Instagram. However, I grew up with traditional media, and there are at least three different news portals that I visit on a daily basis. The stories on these portals are curated by journalists, and I specifically choose media outlets that reflect a broad spectrum of insights and opinions. For many within the younger generations, social media is the only media — there is nothing else. They may encounter clips or information snippets from traditional media outlets, but always through the filter of their social channels.

Traditional media has always served as a basic fact-checking threshold, selecting which news stories make it into a newspaper or broadcast. This role is unavoidable because not everything that happens can be reported. Social media, on the other hand, has no gatekeepers, meaning every piece of news is spread. This opens the door for fake news and conspiracy theories. For instance, the claim that people vaccinated twice against COVID-19 become magnetic would never have made it into a reputable newspaper. Journalists would have known that magnets won't stick to the skin without adhesion. However, this filter does not exist on social media. There, any nonsense can be effortlessly spread as "news."[23]

Increasingly, research shows that false stories have a higher chance of getting shared on a wider scale. A research team that looked at 126,000 rumors spread by three million people found that false stories had six times the retweeting rate on Twitter (now known as X) compared to true stories. The authors of the study interpreted their results as confirming that people are "more likely to share novel information." Whether it is fact or fiction is of lesser interest.[24] As we will explore later in this book, organizations are not powerless against misinformation. They can construct a narrative moat, and there are strategies to counteract and alter false narratives.

While the spread of false stories is a potential threat to companies, there is one other aspect that might be even more challenging. It is very hard to stand out amid the overwhelming amount of content, which is often explicitly designed to entertain and to create high user engagement. Getting through requires a unique point of view and adding real value to topics the audience cares about. Most organizations struggle to get noticed, especially when they treat social media like just another channel, using uninspired press releases, product presentations, or impersonal corporate language.

Social media is fundamentally a platform that works better for individuals than organizations. Only well-known brands can rely on their brand power and focus on it as a communications persona. For everybody else, it might be much more effective to engage their audience through their leaders or influencers as individuals who are associated with a company or brand. This process is not easy for many leaders because it leads them outside their comfort zone. For instance, authentic videos with lower production quality have better engagement on social media.[25] However, it's incredibly challenging for leaders, who are used to controlling their information and communication environment, to now appear naturally on digital platforms. Therefore, those managing an organization's reputation must adapt to this change, encouraging leaders to be more relatable and engaging in order to remain relevant and heard.

On the bright side, whoever can adapt to this new reality can leverage the immense power of social platforms. A great example comes from

Terence Reilly, the president of Stanley, a producer of steel drinkware and food storage products. A woman posted a video on TikTok showing her burned Kia with a Stanley tumbler inside that survived the fire relatively unscathed. The video, which went viral with over 90 million views, showed the interior of the car severely damaged by the fire, but the Stanley tumbler almost pristine. Remarkably, it still had ice in it after the blaze. Reilly responded to the video with a pledge to replace her vehicle. Stanley received very positive feedback and over 40 million views of the president's highly relatable and empathetic video.[26]

Moreover, Stanley utilized their time in the spotlight to promote their completely revamped brand. Initially, when the brand first emerged over a century ago, the stainless steel bottles were primarily marketed to blue-collar workers. However, the company made a strategic decision to rebrand with colors aimed at female consumers, while also leveraging platforms like TikTok to reach their audience. By introducing an element of exclusivity through limited availability, Stanley not only achieved remarkable success through their marketing efforts but also tapped into a new audience who eagerly sought out the new colors following the viral video.

4. Employees want their work to have meaning

It's easier to start a hard company than an easy company.

This is a quote by Sam Altman, the CEO of ChatGPT maker OpenAI. Before OpenAI, Altman served as the president of the renowned startup incubator Y Combinator and gave a lot of presentations about the secrets of successful companies. Why does he think that it's easier to start a hard company? Altman explains:

> The most precious commodity in the startup ecosystem right now is talented people, and for the most part talented people want to work on something they find meaningful.... An easy startup is a headwind; a hard startup is a tailwind. If people care about your success because you seem committed to doing something significant, it's a background force helping you with hiring, advice, partnerships, fundraising, etc.[27]

According to the Edelman Trust Barometer, 69 percent of employees agree that making a societal impact is a strong expectation or deal breaker when considering a job.[28] Creating meaning for its members has become a key success factor for any organization. Meaning can come from many sources, such as enjoying working in a great team. Another key source of meaning is the vision, which outlines the future the organization is working towards, beyond profit-making. If you are confused about vision, mission, and purpose, don't worry, you're not alone. Narratives are a great help in untangling and clarifying these concepts, as you will see in Chapter 5.

The priority level of employee communications has been evolving over the years, further fueled by the COVID crisis and the resulting fundamental changes in how and where we work. In the 2023 Edelman Future of Corporate Communications Study, chief communications officers ranked "Employee Engagement" as their work's most important business outcome, surpassing traditional priorities like enhancing brand reputation and securing positive media coverage.[29]

This highlights the fact that organizations clearly see building a strong internal identity as a top priority, recognizing that reputation is built from the inside out. Employees, being closest to value creation, are most likely to advocate for the company and are often the first to raise concerns. Their experiences and assessments radiate outwards, influencing consumers, media, regulators, activists, and the public.

So let's get back to our example from the beginning of this chapter. Looking at the SVB collapse we can see that all four reputation management catalysts contributed to it. The bank faced unprecedented change, initially triggered by massive capital inflows from startups during COVID-19 and later by the rapid increase in interest rates by the Federal Reserve. In retrospect, the missteps are clear, but the inherent nature of change is its unpredictability and the difficulty of recognizing its patterns until viewed in hindsight.

SVB focused on positioning value narratives for its key audience: startups and innovative companies. Beyond that, SVB was building a variety of narratives on its Environmental, Social, and Governance (ESG) agenda.

However, in the 2022 51-page ESG report, only one page is concerned with risk management.[30] As discussed earlier, the bank failed to build reputational capital around its risk management, and based on the Fed's insights, this external lack of reputation was caused by an insufficient internal risk management culture.[31]

Finally, social media accelerated the crisis once their reputation was attacked and rumors grew. When news broke on that Thursday, there were countless messages and stories about the SVB crisis on Twitter. SVB failed to react to these rumors and had a near-zero own share of voice (SOV) in social media during that day. At some point, people were no longer sharing the original story — SVB seems to be in financial trouble and is trying to raise more capital — but instead shared an emerging narrative represented in this tweet from founder Howard Lerman: "OK I am hearing from dozens of founders about what to do at SVB. It's an all out bank run."[32]

NARRATIVES BUILD REPUTATION

> *Your brand is what people say about you when you're not in the room.*
> — Jeff Bezos

How do you manage reputation? Is reputation even manageable at all? John Doorley and Helio Fred Garcia write in their book *Reputation Management*:

> One reason so many organizations — from corporations, to governments, religions, universities and nonprofits — continue to set records for destroying their own reputations is that they think of reputation as unmanageable.[33]

There was a belief that reputation is hard to manage because it is intangible, hard to grasp conceptually, difficult to measure, and seemingly resistant to influence. However, research has helped to demystify this concept, and we now know that a company's reputation can be quantified, objectives can be set, and strategies can be developed. Ideally, these strategies aim to align stakeholders' perceptions more closely with the company's true identity.

The reason why reputation is still hard to manage comes from two simple but substantial challenges. First, reputational capital has to be built before it's needed. A chemicals company will find itself the focus of public attention if there is a gas leakage. They will need experienced leaders and communicators to retain the public's trust in such a crisis. But most of the time, there is no crisis, and companies face the opposite problem: an ignorant public that does not care about the organization's efforts to build a reputation of operational excellence and environmental protection.

Once I reach the point where I need a new bike and start actively researching options, I will likely already have a few brands in mind that I will consider first. I like lightweight bikes that are easy to carry up steps, so any brand that has built a reputation around this feature will get my attention. Likewise, when employees start looking for new growth opportunities, they may have a few employers in mind that stand out in terms of their reputation for being a great place to grow their careers. In all these cases, reputational capital must be built before it is needed.

The second reason why reputation appears so hard to manage is that it needs to be built in the minds of stakeholders. But how can you build a consistent image about a topic in somebody else's mind, and how do you get their attention in the first place? Whoever intends to manage reputation needs to solve both pieces of this puzzle.

Attention has become increasingly scarce in today's fast-paced and information-saturated world. As a consequence, many businesses have started to use storytelling as a way to capture and hold the attention of their stakeholders. The problem is that stories are individual pieces of information that might resonate with an audience, but a company has many stories, many audiences, and many channels. If these stories don't make sense together, then there is no way a consistent reputation can be formed in the minds of stakeholders.

Consequently, corporate communication must expend significantly more energy to manage coherence. If the product advertising fails to match the behavior from customer service, the campaign will not match the tonality of community management. If crisis communication does not match the investor promises of the CEO, then real problems will arise.

This is the point at which narratives come into play.

Narratives provide a cohesive context to individual stories, linking them in a way that makes sense of the whole and forms a bigger picture. While stories can be impactful, they are often isolated. Narratives tie these stories together, creating a more comprehensive and understandable portrayal of the organization.

Story and narrative are often used interchangeably, but they are distinct concepts. As the Narrative Initiative, a multidisciplinary team of narrative practitioners, explains, "What tiles are to mosaics, stories are to narratives. The relationship is symbiotic: stories bring narratives to life by making them relatable and accessible, while narratives infuse stories with deeper meaning."[34]

Narratives enable strategic control over the organization's reputation. While individual stories are important components of the way in which an organization is perceived, narratives offer a more consistent, coherent, and practical approach to reputation management.

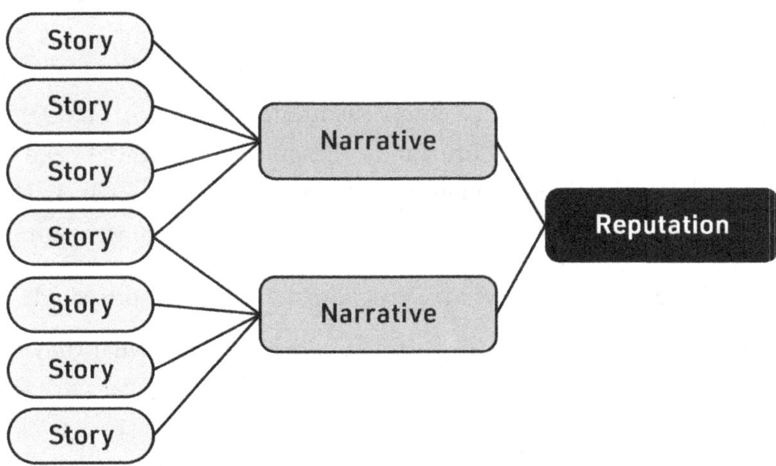

Understanding narratives creates more insights about what drives the reputation of an organization and how this process can be managed more proactively.

An organization will have many narratives. The goal is to define the key strategic ones that are driving reputation. Let's look at an example from

Google and a narrative first introduced with the corporate code of conduct in 2000: "Don't be evil." Google's sheer power and access to data from all aspects of our lives made it a good idea to put this narrative front and center of their organizational reputation.

Over the years, many stories around Google have helped to reinforce this narrative. Google has made various decisions to protect user privacy and data with strong encryption standards and transparency about government requests for user information. In 2010, Google made the decision to stop censoring search results in China, leading to a direct confrontation with the Chinese government and a significant impact on Google's business there. Google has contributed to the open-source community, releasing and supporting various projects. This aligns with a philosophy of openness and sharing knowledge, which can be seen as part of their ethical approach.[35]

All these individual stories contributed to the "Don't be evil" narrative. They allowed Google to build up a strong reputation as an ethical company with a high reputation for social responsibility.[36]

But "Don't be evil" is just one of several underlying narratives that have shaped Google's reputation over time. The overall reputation of an organization can be broken down into sub-areas. One of the best-known models, grounded in extensive research, is the Reputation Quotient® (RQ) model, first published by Charles Fombrun and colleagues in 1999. It has been widely adopted by businesses and academics for reputation assessment. It is based on six dimensions which are the building blocks of a company's reputation:[37]

1. **Emotional Appeal:** How much a company is liked and trusted.
2. **Products and Services:** The quality and reliability of what they sell.
3. **Vision and Leadership:** How inspiring and innovative their leaders are.
4. **Workplace Environment:** If it's a great place to work.
5. **Financial Performance:** How financially strong and stable they are.
6. **Social Responsibility:** Their efforts in making the world a better place.

Using this model as a foundation, here are a few key narratives that serve as building blocks for Google's reputation.

Value narratives like the clean, user-friendly interface and the exceptional speed of all Google services play into the reputation of Google products. Key narratives for Google investors and shareholders are technology leadership and diversification. Google continuously invests in cutting-edge innovations like advancements in search algorithms or artificial intelligence. The diversification narrative highlights the company's growth potential beyond its core search business. Google has diversified into a wide range of sectors, including cloud computing, hardware, mobile operating systems (Android), digital content (YouTube), self-driving cars (Waymo), and healthcare technology.

While a company might have many narratives, there is one singular, most important narrative: the North Star. It contributes to the vision and leadership dimension and radiates across all areas of reputation. It is the fundamental reason a company exists beyond just making money. A strong organization always has a destination. Something promising and new that attracts employees, customers, and investors. A great North Star narrative is able to express what the organization aspires to achieve long term. It can be crafted through concepts like vision and mission, ensuring that all employees work towards the same goals.

Google's North Star is its mission to organize the world's information and make it universally accessible and useful. While the North Star narrative is very influential for all stakeholders, it is most important for employees.

Apple founder Steve Jobs said: "The greatest people are self-managing — they don't need to be managed. Once they know what to do, they'll go figure out how to do it. What they need is a common vision. And that's what leadership is: having a vision; being able to articulate that so the people around you can understand it."[38] Strong narratives help to focus attention and align employees on the topics that the company cares about.

I stressed earlier that reputation needs to be built from the inside out, and that's exactly what narratives achieve. They influence an organization's internal alignment, culture, and identity in the same way they influence the opinions of external stakeholders.

The umbrella term I use in this book for all narratives except the North Star is the **Narrative Moat**.

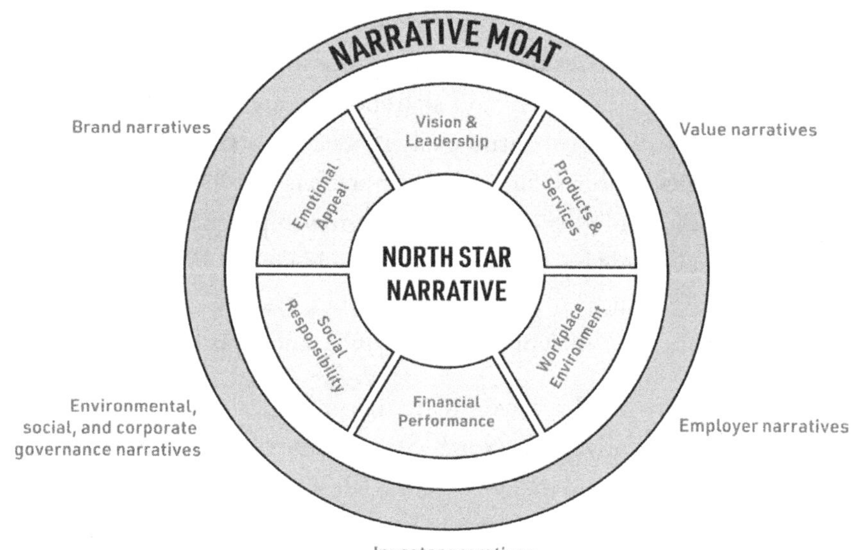

Overview of reputational dimensions and examples of their connected narratives. The North Star narrative influences all narratives and dimensions but primarily connects to the Vision & Leadership reputational dimension.

Is Google's "Don't be evil" narrative now a part of the North Star, or is it one of the social responsibility narratives? Both options are valid. If a core company value is crucial to the company's identity, it might be seen as part of the North Star. There is no right or wrong answer in this case, and each organization can build its own narrative model. In recent years, Google has moved the "Don't be evil" narrative to the background. It is still part of the code of conduct but has been moved to the last line: "And remember … don't be evil, and if you see something that you think isn't right — speak up!"

The narrative perspective offers unique insights into the reputational landscape of an organization. Why is the rise of tools like ChatGPT from OpenAI such a big deal for Google? Because it challenges Google's key narratives on multiple levels.

Investors started to be uncertain about Google's technological leadership, and questions arose about the extent to which AI might threaten the cash cow of search advertising. Value narratives towards customers were challenged as Google Bard didn't yet seem on par with OpenAI's ChatGPT.

Even the "Don't be evil" narrative has come into question, as it has led to Google holding back many of its AI innovations over the years. It now appears that this culture has slowed the company down. The "Don't be evil" narrative has also led Google to contribute to many open-source projects, creating a lot of transparency about their research. In 2017, Google released an AI research paper entitled "Attention is all you need," which is seen today as the key breakthrough for Large Language Models and generative AI. Competitors like OpenAI used these insights to build the AI models that are now challenging Google. There will surely be discussions inside Google on how open they should be to sharing future technological breakthroughs.[39]

Finally, generative AI, in particular, challenges Google's North Star narrative. While AI is surely helpful in organizing the world's information and making it accessible, generative AI is all about the unlimited creation of new content and the interpretation of information. We do not yet know what the long-term impact of this change will mean for how we use technology. We have all seen how social media, initially a welcome tool for bringing us closer together, has now fragmented and polarized the digital world into endless echo chambers. AI will surely keep Google on its toes, both technologically and in how Google's culture, identity, and narratives will have to adapt.

NARRATIVES – TO INFLUENCE OR TO MANIPULATE?

With great power comes great responsibility. Stories have power, and as we will see, narratives can be even more powerful. Narratives are like knives that can be used for meaningful purposes, such as cutting food, but can also be deployed destructively. Similarly, narratives are a kind of universal tool that can be used for a wide variety of purposes. Joachim Weimann is a German economist researching the role of narratives in behavioral and environmental economics. He has written a book about using narratives in public discourse entitled: *Simply Too Simple: How Easy Solutions Threaten Our Democracy.* He writes:

> Focusing on the positive aspects, it's not an exaggeration to say that narratives are the glue that holds societies together. However, focusing on the negative aspects, it's equally true that narratives have played a significant role in the greatest crimes of human history and that these crimes could not have been committed without them.[40]

Weimann posits that narratives play a crucial role in directing human focus to vital topics, simplifying them for broader comprehension. Given the comparatively low demand for information when viewed against the preference for entertainment, those seeking to inform and provide solutions must tailor their communication. This involves crafting messages that are both succinct and easily digestible to effectively engage an audience. Weimann warns about the destructive power of narratives and emphasizes that especially false and oversimplified narratives have a natural advantage:

> Unfortunately, bad narratives have a structural advantage over good ones. It's like the competition between lies and the truth. Lies have the advantage of not being bound to the truth. They can behave much more flexibly, adapt to the circumstances, and thus use every cover. Therefore, bad narratives often have the upper hand when competing for the audience's attention against a good narrative.[41]

Peter Brooks, an American literary theorist, wrote the book *Seduced by Story* discussing how storytelling has crept into every aspect of public discourse.

Brooks argues: "The universe is not our stories about the universe, even if those stories are all we have. Swamped in story as we seem to be, we may lose the distinction between the two, asserting the dominion of our constructed realities over the real thing."[42] He argues that the approach of "best story wins" leads to a competition of storytelling and not a competition of facts. But even Brooks agrees that the "facts on the ground" are simply not as apparent until we make them into a narrative.

Storytelling in business is a dual-edged sword: it can be used to inspire and persuade or to mislead and control. Ethical storytelling requires using narratives to connect emotionally, present ideas, and inspire by aligning with shared values and goals. However, storytelling can also be manipulative, using exaggeration or deception to control or mislead. Understanding narratives thoroughly is key to mitigating their potential harm. Ethical leaders need to focus on transparency, integrity, and accountability in their narratives, ensuring they align with the values of the organization and the key stakeholders.

2. STORIES WIN GAMES, NARRATIVES WIN CHAMPIONSHIPS

WHEN EVEN BECKHAM COULDN'T BEND IT

It's June 2016 and the world's gaze is firmly fixed on the United Kingdom. The country is on the brink of a momentous decision: the highly anticipated Brexit referendum to decide whether to remain a member of the European Union (EU) or to exit. Polls paint a close picture, with 51 percent favoring the "Remain in the EU" campaign and 49 percent for the "Vote Leave" campaign. Alarmingly for Remainers, momentum appears to be shifting towards leaving.

The Remain campaign had built its case around the fear of a post-Brexit economic decline. Countless business leaders, experts, and foreign dignitaries were mobilized to warn of the destructive effects Brexit could have on UK businesses. Even United States President Barack Obama, during a visit to the UK, debunked the Vote Leave promise of favorable bilateral trade agreements post-Brexit, noting that the UK would find itself at the "back of the queue" once it left the EU.

Nevertheless, these economic apprehensions resonated only to a point. Even worse, the voters and the media were showing real signs of fear fatigue. The economic argument had been overused and was no longer resonating in the final weeks of the respective campaigns. Instead, the focus of discussions and media attention had shifted to the other pivotal Brexit issue: immigration.[1]

The UK had experienced a significant increase in immigration from Eastern Europe in the years since the EU's eastern expansion in 2004. This surge posed challenges for housing, healthcare, and wages, particularly for lower-income British families. The central message of the Leave campaign was the need to "take back control" of immigration, and polls consistently showed that immigration was becoming the decisive issue in the Brexit referendum.

Luckily, the Remain campaign still held a trump card. Forty-eight hours before the referendum, David Beckham, the former captain of England's football team and a national icon, publicly voiced his support for EU membership. In a personal Instagram post, he reflected on the enriching nature of foreign cultures, recounting his own journey to success at his boyhood club, Manchester United, playing alongside France's Eric Cantona and Denmark's Peter Schmeichel.[2]

Beckham also remarked on the privilege of playing and living in Madrid, Milan, and Paris with teammates from all around Europe and the world. Beckham concluded his post with an emotional message for unity: "For our children and their children, we should face the world's problems together, not alone."

Having Beckham endorse the Remain campaign just hours before the referendum was a big deal. Focus group research had been showing that voters put immigration at the center of the Brexit debate.[3] Yet Britons were confused and frustrated, not knowing whose opinion they could trust. Would Beckham's last-minute, high-profile message resonate and shift the momentum back to the Remain team? After all, the polls were neck and neck, and the final results could come down to just a few thousand votes.

Two days later, on June 23, 2016, the Leave campaign emerged victorious, securing a 52 percent win in the referendum. The next day I found myself discussing what had happened with Staffbase cofounder Martin Böhringer.

He had just returned from London, where he frequently traveled to meet investors and customers. Not for one moment did he expect the UK citizens to vote like they did. What had happened? And why were we and a lot of the people around us being taken by surprise like this? One of the reasons was that the Leave campaign had proven particularly successful at engaging individuals who had never before voted. The campaign managed to alleviate concerns about economic decline while taking control of the immigration narrative, an area where the Remain campaign fell disastrously short.

Was immigration the only issue contributing to the Remain campaign's defeat? Definitely not. British journalists Jason Farrell and Paul Goldsmith list 18 reasons for the Brexit decision in their book *How to Lose A Referendum*. Some of these reasons stretch back into history, such as Britain's absence from the Treaty of Rome, which brought about the creation of the European Economic Community in 1957. Nonetheless, they unequivocally highlight the immigration debate as the final tipping point for the Brexit vote, noting, "It was in late May 2016 that [Remain] lost control of the campaign. The centre of gravity of the argument shifted from the economy to immigration, and the polls shifted with it."[4]

The Remain team had brought together plenty of stories and arguments on immigration. But they lacked an overarching and coherent message regarding this pivotal issue, along with the resulting narrative such messaging would have created. A great story alone cannot change hearts and minds, but a strong narrative can. If we want to understand why David Beckham's story failed to resonate with voters, we need to better understand the difference between stories and narratives and how they relate to each other.

STORIES HELP US MAKE SENSE OF THE WORLD

From birth, our brains begin to understand the world by forming cause-and-effect relationships. In other words, we learn to think, "If this happens, then that happens." Our brains are constantly searching for ways to make sense of what we experience and encounter. It's the reason toddlers never get tired of asking why. This survival mechanism is deeply rooted in our brains because we need to understand the threats that surround us.

Stories help immensely. They give our brains a shortcut to understanding cause-and-effect relationships without having to experience potentially dangerous situations ourselves. I love hiking in the mountains, but there are certain dangers that every hiker needs to be aware of. We tend to underestimate how altitude differences can add to the difficulty of a hike or how quickly changing weather can affect our journey. All these challenges can lead to countless complex scenarios. Sitting in a mountain hut with fellow hikers and talking about past tours is not just fun, but also instructive. Usually, people will share stories about the challenges they have encountered that put them in difficult, and sometimes dangerous, situations. These stories allow us to collect a mental list of potential problems and solutions.[5] Based on these scenarios, I can mentally play out a hiking tour before I start. From listening to the stories of other hikers, I've learned to always pack rain gear, a fully charged phone, and enough food and water.

Stories have power. They can inspire, challenge, entertain, and teach us. A story is a finite tale about specific events and individuals that is typically told from beginning to middle to end. It often revolves around characters with whom the reader or listener can easily identify. I have two daughters and I have witnessed firsthand how much more they connect with female heroes like Anna in Frozen compared to male heroes in other movies. Neuroscientific research has revealed that emotionally engaging stories can trigger attention and the release of oxytocin, a hormone linked to empathy. It was found that a good story structure, which sustains attention and emotional connection, could predict behaviors, such as donating to charity, with 82 percent accuracy.[6]

Our brains are naturally drawn to stories because of the feelings they inspire, such as empathy, excitement, love, and suspense. That's why we spend so much time watching or reading stories in our everyday lives, sometimes even getting hooked on them through streaming services or social media.

The Brexit referendum was a hugely consequential decision for Great Britain. Stories gave the average voter a number of very different perspectives on the possible repercussions of leaving the EU. Scottish fishermen, Welsh coal miners, London bankers, and the US president each had their own perspective about the opportunities and challenges of membership in the European Union. Both campaign teams used the emotional power and appeal of stories to convince voters to support their respective arguments.

David Beckham's Instagram post was one story among many that were created and shared in the course of the Brexit debate. During the 2016 campaigns, every potential British voter heard countless such stories from family, friends, colleagues, TV, radio, newspapers, and social media.

Great stories are the ultimate emotional currency. They can attract people to a topic and convince them to agree with a certain perspective or point of view. However, the moment a voter stepped into the voting booth to be confronted with the choice to remain or leave, it's safe to say that there would be no way to recount every single story they'd encountered throughout the campaign. Instead, voters would have already made up their minds by constructing these stories into something else: narratives.

NARRATIVES ARE PATTERNS THAT EMERGE FROM STORIES

4, 8, 16, __

January, February, March, _____

Chances are, while reading the sequences above, you were able to complete the pattern quickly. That's because our brains are particularly good at identifying patterns. When we find ourselves in new surroundings or encounter new experiences, our brains search our stored memories for similar information and experiences. Recognizing known patterns helps us quickly understand situations and react accordingly.

As we have seen, stories help us to imagine alternative solutions to potentially challenging problems. Pattern recognition goes one step further, helping us to summarize various stories into a common narrative.

For example, through their encounters with bears, our early ancestors learned to recognize the sound of a bear's roar and associate it with danger. Although every roar of a bear might sound a little different, our ancestors couldn't afford to stop and think about each encounter as a new experience. Their brains recognized the pattern and they started telling each other, "Watch out if you hear a roar because this might be the sound of a dangerous bear!" This is a narrative. It's the connecting thread of multiple stories that leads to a broader understanding or conclusion.

This narrative gave our ancestors a shared understanding of their world: bears are dangerous, but there is a way to know when one is near you. It's an important evolutionary advantage. It helps the tribe survive by avoiding potential danger. Our ancestors didn't need to personally experience a dangerous encounter with a bear; they learned from the narrative that emerged from the collected stories of their tribe members.

What was true for our ancestors is true today. We organize everything that happens to us and give it meaning through patterns. These patterns are called personal narratives. The psychologist Jerome Bruner was the first to speak about the cognitive power of these personal narratives. According to him, we give sense, meaning, and direction to each and every event and experience we have. We're writing our own stories and building our own narratives.[7,8]

New brain imaging technology can even point to a specific part of the brain as the storytelling hub: the hippocampus. A study by the Center for Neuroscience at the University of California in 2021 shows that we find it easier to remember events when they're part of an overarching narrative. Co-author Dr. Brendan Cohn-Sheehy explains, "Things that happen in real life don't always connect directly, but we can remember the details of each event better if they form a coherent narrative."[9]

The study asked volunteers to learn and recall a series of short stories.

These stories, created specifically for the study, featured an event with main and side characters. They were constructed so that some formed connected, two-part narratives while others did not.

The researchers played recordings of the stories to the volunteers, who were placed inside a magnetic resonance imaging (MRI) scanner. The next day, they scanned the volunteers again while they recalled the stories. The researchers compared the different activity patterns recorded in the hippocampus between hearing and recalling the stories.

The result was that they saw more similar brain activity for learning pieces of a coherent story than for stories that did not connect. In other words, we find it easier to remember events when they fit into an overarching narrative.[9]

FRAMING CONNECTS STORIES AND NARRATIVES

Stories can be connected to narratives through the use of framing. The term "framing" was originally coined by social scientist Gregory Bateson in 1972, and it refers to the ways in which we present information to influence the perceptions of others. Framing can dictate which aspects of a story are highlighted and the manner in which they are interpreted. By concentrating on specific themes, perspectives, or angles across multiple stories, framing plays a significant role in the development of narratives.

Framing is sometimes viewed negatively as a means to distort information, but we all unconsciously frame stories all the time. It is an essential aspect of communication to reduce complexity. Consider the example of the bear mentioned earlier and imagine a hunter sitting at the campfire and telling a story about his encounter with it. He will naturally omit many of the mundane details and frame the story in a way that holds the listeners' attention by focusing on the exciting or dangerous parts.[10]

David Beckham framed his personal story and success as a result of playing together with great players from other European countries and concluded that the future is better built together and not alone. However, the Leave side demonstrated how Beckham's story could be reframed.

Leave had created a narrative about a UK elite who were reaping all the benefits of free trade and the lowered wages caused by high immigration numbers while the working class struggled to keep up. According to this "haves and the have-nots" point of view, one could look at Beckham's story as proof of elite privilege. Only people like David Beckham could afford to live in Paris, Milan, and Madrid and experience the bright side of European multicultural life.

Secretary of State for Justice and Leave supporter Michael Gove said about Beckham's message, "As a QPR [West London football club Queens Park

Rangers] fan, I know what it's like to support the underdog anyway." Gove used framing to link a powerful story from the Remain campaign to one of the core narratives of the Leave campaign.[11]

Closely related to framing is the agenda-setting theory. In fact, framing is sometimes also referred to as *second-level agenda setting*. While framing influences how information is presented and interpreted, agenda setting suggests that public opinion can already be shaped by determining *what* issues are given the most attention in news coverage. A common example of agenda setting is focusing on the violent aspects of a political protest rather than the arguments behind why the protest is taking place.

Agenda setting and framing have the potential to be manipulative and are the subject of extensive research on how media organizations and journalists use these techniques to influence public opinion. However, manipulating something in a particular direction does not necessarily imply bad intentions. For example, it could inspire an audience to quit smoking or spend more time with their children. Framing and agenda setting are tools, and like all tools, they are not inherently good or bad; it is how we use them that matters.

SEVEN NARRATIVE VIRTUES

Narratives are not just different from stories — they are in many ways much more powerful. Let's use a simple example to illustrate the power of narratives in our thinking.

Despite the rising popularity of streaming, I still love going to the cinema. But since I only go to the movies a few times a year, I want to be sure that the movie I choose to see in a theater is one I'm really going to enjoy. I spend a lot of time researching beforehand, reading reviews, and asking others for their opinions.

When *Barbie* was released in 2023, I was certain it wasn't even worth considering. However, my perspective began to change with the first review I read online. To my surprise, it described the movie as not just for kids but as having a really empowering plot and subversive storytelling. The next perspective came from my teenage daughter, who had seen the movie. Not only had the film thoroughly surprised her, she liked it so much that she wanted to tell me all about it. Then, I heard about the *Barbie* movie's ongoing box office success, which defied all expectations, becoming the most commercially successful movie in the history of Warner Bros. Finally, an unexpected endorsement came from the host of a stock market podcast I listen to regularly. He's a man about my age who highly recommended the movie.

What happened here was a gradual change in my perception of a movie I had not yet seen. Individual stories and events were reshaping my personal narrative about the movie. At that point, my brain created a narrative as a blueprint or summary of these stories. It was something like: *The* Barbie *movie isn't what you think it is and it might be worth watching.*

One can argue that box office revenues are not really stories but actual factual information. This is true, and Jerome Bruner made a distinction between two modes of thinking to make sense of the world: the paradigmatic (or logico-scientific) mode, which uses logic and evidence to build cause-and-effect relationships, and the narrative mode, which constructs stories to make sense of experiences.[12]

While the former seeks "truth" through empirical evidence and logical deduction, like Box Office revenues, narratives are concerned with lifelikeness or "verisimilitude." In other words, a good narrative rings true by resonating with our experiences and understanding of the world, whether or not it's factually accurate.

Logical evidence and narratives can form a powerful combination to help people make sense of the world. A business would be unable to operate based on stories alone, as factual information like quarterly numbers or annual reports needs to be shared with stakeholders. Equally, the entire absence of stories would leave an organization as a cold, mechanistic entity without a compelling purpose or an exciting future direction.

Focusing on the narrative rather than just individual pieces of information and stories is immensely powerful. Therefore, a specific question I continuously returned to during the research for this book was how to understand which characteristics differentiate narratives from stories. Here are some of the most important and distinctive features of narratives that are crucial for grasping the essence of effective communication:

1. Narratives are the basis for action

Narratives focus our attention and motivate action. We have a limited field of attention, and narratives act as a filter for which topics we should concentrate on. The emerging Barbie narrative in my mind created more focus on this particular movie. As we will discuss in Chapter 7, the simultaneous release of *Barbie* and *Oppenheimer* and all of the resulting "Barbenheimer" memes built even more buzz around both movies. The loser was Tom Cruise's *Mission Impossible — Dead Reckoning*, which launched days before and was completely overshadowed by the other two movies.

Just as narratives can guide our attention, they can also channel our motives and direct our willpower towards a specific point or particular action. They do this because they highlight causal relationships. For example, I observed from others who went to the cinema that they came back and were positively surprised. The more stories I heard that reinforced this narrative the more I wanted to go and experience the surprise myself.

Whether it's a political campaign like Brexit, the decision to go to a movie, buy a car, join a company, or support an organizational change initiative, narratives drive action, and that's what ultimately counts.[13]

2. Narratives are inclusive – it's about me

Stories are mostly about what happened to other people. My daughter spoke about her visit to the cinema. She might be a great storyteller who can get my attention and make an emotional connection, but her story never becomes mine. On the other hand, narratives are inclusive — they can become about me. The more I learn about a movie the more I might consider watching it myself. That's why narratives are so powerful, because while stories are about other people's experiences, narratives invite each of us to be participants.

What works for everyday decisions like watching a movie also works for much bigger decisions in our lives. A narrative can serve as a highly effective tool for providing a long-term sense of direction and opportunity, as well as motivating and mobilizing people to take action in pursuit of that opportunity. Narratives can create movements. Stories, in turn, can be a particularly powerful way to build credibility for the narrative by highlighting individuals who have taken action and showcasing the impact they have made.

3. Narratives are open-ended

Narratives are systems of stories, some resolved and some not. This definition comes from narrative researcher Steven R. Corman, a professor of strategic communication at Arizona State University. He states, "It is the 'systemness' of a narrative that makes it open-ended because new stories can always develop that relate to other stories in the system, thus providing an ongoing basis for interpreting events and motivating behavior."[14]

In my mind, the narrative of the *Barbie* movie evolved from considering it a children's film to acknowledging that it might surpass my expectations. Since narratives are open-ended, the prevailing narrative three years from now remains uncertain. Perhaps it will be regarded as one of the most iconic movies of the 2020s, or it could mark the inglorious beginning of an endless series of *Barbie* movie sequels and prequels. Another angle of a future narrative may come from the controversial Oscar nominations. The blockbuster was nominated in eight categories, including best picture. Actor Ryan Gosling, who plays Ken in the movie, was also nominated for best supporting actor. However, lead actress Margot Robbie and director Greta Gerwig were not nominated, which provoked numerous outraged reactions.

This openness of narrative makes it ideal for organizations to use as their strategic North Star. It is able to change and evolve. That is why a specific founding story of a company doesn't make for a good mission or vision statement unless it plays into a larger narrative of what an organization aspires to create.

4. Narratives grow stronger with every story

Narratives are built from various stories and factual information. They can grow over time and embed deeply into the identity and culture of their audience. Every fitting story reinforces the narrative. Remember the story about Stanley, the stainless steel bottles now aimed at female consumers? Every time people see someone use a Stanley bottle, be it their neighbor, classmate, or a famous celebrity, it contributes to the narrative that this seems to be a trend. In a world of limited attention, narratives are a more reliable and ultimately more powerful way to convey messages.

Some stories resonate deeply with audiences and go viral, seemingly changing minds overnight. However, this impact is unpredictable and impossible to plan.

5. Narratives frame stories and create confirmation bias

We previously discussed the idea that stories can be framed in order to construct a certain narrative. The same is true in reverse. Once a narrative exists in our mind, it may change how we perceive new information.

When we come across information that contradicts our existing beliefs, it often leads to cognitive dissonance. This refers to a state of mental discomfort that arises when we hold two conflicting thoughts simultaneously. To alleviate this discomfort, we subconsciously use strategies like confirmation bias. Confirmation bias involves favoring information that confirms a preexisting belief and can manifest in various ways. We might selectively search for information that confirms our beliefs. Or we might interpret ambiguous or neutral information in a way that aligns with our existing beliefs.

For example, after hearing many favorable stories about *Barbie*, I began forming a positive narrative on the merit, value, and quality of the film. But then, I also encountered people who didn't like the movie. How do these inputs factor in? Following the urge to resolve my cognitive dissonance, I might have concluded that someone who didn't like *Barbie* simply isn't receptive to subversive storytelling or falsely interpreted the film as anti-male.

The consequence is that existing narratives are hard to change. Attempting change might even reinforce and deepen current beliefs. Changing narratives is a fascinating topic that I will discuss in much greater detail in Chapter 4.

6. Narratives are how we share our opinions

When people ask me what I think about the *Barbie* movie, I usually say that it surprised me and that I liked it. I might add an actual story like how I didn't want to watch it in the first place. However, the first thing that comes to mind is the narrative.

When people ask for your opinion about famous cities such as Paris, New York, London, Berlin, or Tokyo, you will usually share your key narrative first, followed by a story to illustrate the narrative. The same is true when an employee is asked about their job and employer. They will usually first share their narrative, such as: "It's a cool company, I learn a lot, but it's quite a long commute." This is not a story, it's a narrative.

7. Narratives measure the outcome of communication

Measuring the effectiveness of communication presents a challenge: while it's relatively straightforward to track outputs like individual content pieces and their audience engagement through views, comments, and likes, gauging the outcomes, such as influencing behavior or reputation enhancement, is more complex.

The significant advantage of focusing on narratives lies in their formation within the minds of your audience, which provides a unique opportunity to measure communication outcomes. A simple pulse survey question can evaluate to what degree an audience agrees with a given narrative statement. This strategy benefits communication campaigns by aligning them closely with their desired outcome. By defining the end-state — what the audience should think or feel after the campaign — we can zero in on the essential aspects for the audience to comprehend and remember.

Even the strongest and most emotional stories can only resonate with their audience if they connect to an overarching narrative. For a campaign like

Brexit, there were no good or bad stories. Stories either do or do not support the underlying narrative. The Leave campaign had worked towards creating a narrative for their audience that might be summarized as: *I believe we need to change something about how we handle immigration in the United Kingdom and take back control of our borders. For that, I am willing to accept the potential risk of an economic downside resulting from Brexit.*

What was the Remain campaign's counternarrative regarding immigration? Unfortunately for them, they never developed a coherent immigration narrative that was used consistently. The Brexit vote forced two very different groups, the Conservative Party and the Labour Party, to work together on the Remain campaign. Both parties had very different views on immigration and never managed to develop a consistent perspective on this decisive issue. The Conservatives wanted to limit the number of immigrants. At the same time, Labour politicians either defended their past policy of allowing more immigrants into the UK or simply insisted that there was no issue with immigration at all.

Looking through the narrative lens, we can see that the story from David Beckham had a hard time connecting to an existing positive narrative about immigration — mainly because there wasn't one. Whoever is able to build a communications strategy based on narratives as opposed to individual stories will have a big advantage. As we have seen, narratives are more inclusive, they can grow over time, and they are the basis for action. Even more, once a narrative is established, it will frame every new story that enters the picture.

What would a British voter have told a friend when she was asked, "What's your opinion about staying or leaving?" or "What do you think about immigration?" Thinking about the kinds of messages and stories that support the creation of a desired narrative should have been the focus of the Remain campaign. A message from David Beckham aligned with such a framework would have had a much greater impact.

But what exactly does a narrative look like? Let's first examine a general definition and then provide a concrete approach.

THE STRUCTURE OF A NARRATIVE

According to Jerome Bruner, narratives help us construct meaning by organizing events and experiences into a structure with a beginning, middle, and end. This structure allows us to see relationships and connections between events, making them more understandable. Let's consider for example the classic tale of the underdog. One of the most famous underdog **stories** ever is told in the movie *Rocky*:

- **Beginning:** Rocky Balboa, a boxer from Philadelphia, struggles with life's complexities and his own self-doubt while dreaming of a better future.
- **Middle:** Seizing an unexpected opportunity, Rocky prepares to fight the heavyweight champion, Apollo Creed, undergoing rigorous training that tests his limits and builds his confidence.
- **End:** Rocky goes the distance, losing the fight by a narrow margin but winning the respect of the audience and proving to himself that he has what it takes to be a contender.

The **narrative** behind this underdog story could be summarized like this:

- **Beginning:** The underdog emerges from humble origins, burdened by adversity but marked by unacknowledged potential.
- **Middle:** Through trials and relentless determination, the underdog confronts and overcomes obstacles, undergoing significant personal growth.
- **End:** Culminating in a hard-won triumph, the underdog's journey concludes with a victory that underscores the resilience of the human spirit.

Stories and narratives share common elements, but they differ in their level of abstraction. Stories are very specific, while narratives are more general. For example, story characters like Rocky Balboa are depicted as individuals with distinct personalities. At the narrative level, characters are portrayed more as types of people or groups, such as underdogs. A story about a specific CEO of a UK company warning about the economic consequences of Brexit would involve a specific business leader and a specific company. In contrast, a narrative about the negative economic consequences of leaving the EU would focus on business leaders and experts in general, and their warnings about the negative consequences.

The structure of narratives is sometimes not plain to see and might need a bit of construction. Germany, for instance, has a very strong positive narrative about the Nordics, which includes Scandinavian countries such as Denmark, Norway, and Sweden. This narrative involves unspoiled nature, happier people, and tasteful design. What is the beginning, middle, and end here? This is where, according to narrative researcher Prof. Michael Müller, a bit of "narrative construction" is allowed.[15]

For the Nordics we could think about an initial state where we are stressed out, overworked, and unhappy. The transformation could involve taking a log cabin vacation in Sweden, a fishing trip to Norway, or buying Danish design furniture for your home. It means either going to the Nordics or integrating key values of the Nordic experience, like hygge or natural design, into your own home and life. The supposed end state is a happier life and living closer to nature.

Focusing on just the plot — with a beginning, middle, and end — is still very basic. The reason narratives connect with people emotionally is that they inherit more features from stories than the plot alone. The FrameWorks Institute published a more detailed model of the form of narratives in 2021. Their research was supported by the Bill and Melinda Gates Foundation because the goal was to provide better insight and education about the key role narratives play in social change efforts.[16]

The FrameWorks Institute's model includes three dimensions of narratives:

1. What happens in the story world regarding character, plot, and settings.
2. How the story is told, including the point of view and evaluative judgments.
3. How the story is received with its intended audience and within its cultural and social context.

The following table shows an overview of the dimensions and the individual features of narratives. It's easier to understand the model based on a concrete example. Here, we use the core narrative of the Leave campaign: Take back control.

	FEATURE OF THE NARRATIVE	EXAMPLE: TAKE BACK CONTROL
STORY WORLD	CHARACTERS	The British people
	PLOT	**Start**: We are being patronized by the EU **Transformation**: Voting to leave **End**: Being back in control of our destiny
	SETTING	British communities where life is difficult
STORY TOLD	WHO TELLS THE STORIES?	**Initially**: Right-wing Eurosceptic and anti-immigration groups **Later**: Popular conservative politicians like Boris Johnson join the movement
	EVALUATIVE JUDGMENTS: WHO IS A HERO OR A VILLAIN?	**Villain:** The elite which profits from globalization **Heroes:** Normal people who are being given the once-in-a-lifetime chance to be in control and take back their country
STORY RECEIVED	THE INTENDED AUDIENCE	People with low or middle income
	CULTURAL AND SOCIAL CONTEXT ACTIVATED	Stop the decline from world power to middle power Leading Britain back to its former glory Bring back a time when things felt less complex and the speed of change was slower

As we shift from the context of a story to that of a narrative, the interpretation of "point of view" changes significantly. In a given story, the point of view pertains to specific characters — the plot unfolds through the lens of one or several characters, sometimes changing throughout. In a narrative, the point of view is tied to specific social groups. Essentially, whereas stories are relayed from the perspective of individuals, narratives convey the viewpoint of a specific social group.

The last point in the model — *cultural and social context activated* — touches on a key point of narrative strategies: Narratives do not stand alone but rather connect to the narrative map of their audience. We will dive deeply into this important topic in the next chapter.

Now that we have a basic structure for narratives, we need an approach to finding and formulating them for ourselves.

HOW DO YOU IDENTIFY POWERFUL NARRATIVES?

Andy Raskin is a consultant from San Francisco who helps technology companies to find their strategic narrative. Raskin has a podcast called *The Bigger Narrative*. In each episode, he interviews CEOs of companies to discuss how to use strategic narratives to teach their buyers about an "old world vs. new world" shift in their sector. This approach positions narratives and stories as more than the afterthought of a marketing campaign. In fact, they are the North Star that should guide not only how you talk but also what products you build and/or acquire.

Raskin starts each episode by calling his mother, who is not a tech expert. He sends her the recorded episode and then asks her to sum up with common sense what she learned and understood from the conversation. That's a fun exercise because these companies often have very niche business models addressing needs deep in the tech stack of their customers. This initial conversation is always such an eye-opener about the power of understanding the mind of your potential audience.

You may argue that his mom doesn't represent a potential customer in a business-to-business context and that their buyers will be much more educated about the topics. But that's often not the case. Many buyers are new to a field and are tasked with researching new technology. Even if they understand, they often need to take the buying decision back to their managers or even the CEO. The easier a message is to understand, whether by business buyers or end customers, the better.

Raskin is using this creative approach to make his core point: if you want to communicate effectively, you first need to listen. You need to talk to your audience of employees, investors, or buyers. Only then can you define a differentiated narrative.

An emerging term for this approach is *storylistening*. It refers to the methods dedicated to collecting stories and narratives. Examples of these methods include focus groups and narrative interviews.

The basic attitude here is that of just listening. In contrast to "ordinary" interviews, narrative interviews do not ask questions about the interviewee's opinions or facts, but simply try to encourage them to narrate. But why let them tell stories and not just ask questions — as is usually the case in employee or customer surveys?

When people freely talk about their experiences, it's much easier to gain deep insights into their actual beliefs and behaviors. Questions only elicit opinions and answers that the interviewee believes are desired. For example, if you ask an employee of a company if he is customer-oriented, he can hardly deny it — not being customer-oriented is almost akin to a mortal sin. In general, the respondents also believe in the truth of their answers. But what does it mean when, in 40 narrative interviews from a large company, neither the word "customer" nor the conceptual concept of customer orientation comes up even once? We can safely assume that the company is not actually as customer-centric as they'd like to believe.[17]

Dominic Cummings, the communications lead of the Leave campaign, carried out six focus groups in May 2014 prior to the campaign kickoff. The discussions about the EU were still fresh in the minds of the participants as the focus groups were assembled just after the previous EU elections. Based on these conversations and his own understanding of sentiments towards the EU, Cummings created a communications strategy for the Leave campaign to achieve its objective.

There was a noticeable theme in this report. People felt they'd lost influence over various facets of their lives. The word "control" appeared 37 times in this 19-page report. One focus group participant, a man from Thurrock, just east of London, simply remarked: "We have lost control due to Europe." The phrase "take back control" was spoken five times.

The slogans were practically hand delivered by the focus groups. The Leave campaign would embrace "Vote Leave: Take Back Control" as its central and overarching narrative.[18]

The Remain campaign started much later with their communications team and as a result didn't have time for extensive research and focus groups. Their messages had to be created by agencies and didn't benefit from the stories and narratives of actual voters.

This chapter focused on narratives as patterns in our brains. However, the true power of narratives is unleashed when they transfer from individual minds to the collective consciousness of groups, nations, or even all of humanity. This is one of the most fascinating areas for me, because the deeper you look, the more you realize how much of our thinking, actions, and culture is influenced by narratives. The example we start with in the next chapter comes from an industry that has also sparked many controversial discussions at Staffbase over the past few years: the weapons industry. The key question is: Should we do business with companies that build weapons?

3. THE NARRATIVE LANDSCAPE

TECH'S MOST CONTROVERSIAL STARTUP

Palmer Luckey stands on the stage of the All-In Summit in Miami, wearing his signature Hawaiian shirt. At 30 years old, he is already a legend in the tech industry. He revolutionized the virtual reality space with his Oculus Rift headset and sold the company to Facebook (Meta) in 2014 for $2 billion USD.

His next move though was a surprising one. He founded Anduril Industries, a defense tech company. On the stage in Miami, he talks about a journey that began with a small startup in a space that was, at best, ignored and more often openly questioned ethically:

> The vast majority of conversations we had [with Venture Capital firms] were about whether or not it was even ethically ok to ever build a company that would build weapons, and the people who turned us down ... they thought that it was inherently wrong to

> build tools capable of being used for violence because they believed that the idea of deterring violence through having a strong arsenal was fundamentally obsolete and itself wrong.[1]

He goes on to talk about the continuing negativity from the press, such as a Bloomberg cover story from 2019 calling Anduril "tech's most controversial startup."[2] However, Anduril isn't the only company that has experienced controversies over its investments in defense technology.

For instance, in 2018 Google employees openly opposed and managed to cancel Google's participation in Project Maven, a Pentagon initiative aimed at integrating artificial intelligence into military applications. The employees' petition to Google CEO Sundar Pichai read: "We believe that Google should not be in the business of war. Therefore, we ask that Project Maven be canceled and Google draft, publicize and enforce a clear policy stating that neither Google nor its contractors will ever build warfare technology."[3]

Even though the rise of Silicon Valley in the 1950s was closely connected to working with the Pentagon on high-tech defense contracts, the end of the Cold War fundamentally changed the perception of the defense industry. By 2018, building technology for the defense was largely seen in Silicon Valley as obsolete and unethical.

A key reason for this shift was a powerful narrative created in 1989 by American political scientist Francis Fukuyama in his essay, "The End of History?" Fukuyama suggested that the fall of the Berlin Wall and the collapse of the Soviet Union marked not just the end of the Cold War but also the end of the progression of human ideological evolution. He saw Western liberal democracy as the endpoint of humanity's sociocultural evolution and the final form of human government. There would be no further major ideological evolutions or revolutions in how societies are fundamentally structured.[4]

The developments that Fukuyama pointed out in his influential essay resulted in Western democracies reducing their priority level of defense spending and shifting towards prioritizing economic and social policies within stable democratic frameworks. It also meant that younger generations grew up without ever experiencing the great power competition that characterized the world during the Cold War.

Cracks in the "end of history" narrative started to appear with the 9/11 terror attacks, rising tensions between the US and emerging superpower China over Taiwan, and the 2014 Russian annexation of Crimea. Then a significant moment came on February 24, 2022, when Russia invaded Ukraine. A military and nuclear superpower attacked a neighbor in Europe which was well on its way to becoming a successful liberal democracy.

For most of my life, I would have voted to invest less money into the military. I spent my mandatory military service in a main battle tank brigade of the German armed forces in the 1990s, and these weapons felt obsolete and entirely out of touch with the political situation after the fall of the Wall. A land war which involved many tanks seemed unthinkable. And yet, here we are, more than two decades later, with NATO countries sending much-needed tanks to Ukraine.

The war in Ukraine also revealed another painful reality: the degree to which warfare has changed. It's still high-tech, but it's not about multimillion-dollar F35 fighter jets or modern tanks. What dominates the battlefield are drones. They are much cheaper than traditional equipment — costing just a few hundred dollars per piece — but they can easily take out a tank, destroy an airplane, or guide precision artillery.[5]

This new generation of weapons — some of which are even autonomous now — is being developed everywhere in the world, and US technological leadership is not as superior as it once was. For instance, the biggest drone manufacturer in the world is the Chinese company DJI, which currently dominates more than 70 percent of the global drone market.[6]

In this new world of cheap-but-deadly weapons, software, connected systems, and AI-supported autonomy will play a major role in deciding who prevails in an armed conflict. In the wake of these fundamental changes, Anduril has gone from being an outsider to becoming the poster child of a new kind of defense industry. They use software and AI to build fully connected command and control systems that can coordinate a wide range of air systems and underwater vehicles. The 2022 funding round raised

$1.48 billion USD at a valuation of $8.5 billion USD. Anduril is pioneering the movement, but there are now many more defense startups, and venture capitalists are shifting attention and money toward the space. David Ulevitch, General Partner at venture capital firm Andreessen Horowitz, remarks: "If you believe in democracy, democracy demands a sword."[7]

Anduril and defense technology are great examples of how influential existing narratives are on our thinking and the decisions we make. In contrast to personal narratives, these narratives exist at the societal/cultural level. They provide the frame and the material to form our personal narratives.

Do you think a strong military is expensive, that it only escalates conflicts, and that it's unethical to build weapons capable of killing humans? Or do you believe that a strong military helps a country to protect itself, acting as a powerful deterrent that avoids conflict and war? You may say that the answer to this question depends on your values and beliefs. But what underlies your values and beliefs? The answer is your own narrative landscape, shaped by the environment and culture in which you grew up and the experiences you have had over the course of your life.

NARRATIVES ARE OUR CULTURAL LENS

Humans know and share thousands of narratives. One important way to bring order to this multitude is to group them along a dimension that can best be summarized as "cultural embeddedness." This concept refers to how deeply a narrative is anchored in the culture and identity of a group of people. New narratives, known only to a minority audience, can be considered *emerging narratives*. Once they become deeply embedded in the collective mind of a group, these narratives turn into *master narratives*.

Most stories that are told on the major news channels either nationally or globally will create emerging narratives. One well-known and ever-evolving narrative is the monetary policy of the Federal Reserve System, also known as the Fed. Whenever the Fed chair talks about the Fed's view of current monetary conditions and changes to interest rates, the global market listens very carefully.

Even though emerging narratives are widespread, this does not mean they are deeply embedded in the culture of the audience. For instance, the current Federal Reserve narrative of stable or soon-to-be falling interest rates will soon be old news and replaced with a new emerging Fed narrative. However other emerging narratives like the 9/11 terrorist attacks quickly turned into master narratives as they became deeply embedded in the collective memory of not only a nation but the entire world.

The "end of history" master narrative can also be traced back to a pivotal event: the fall of the Berlin Wall and the end of the Cold War. An example of its impact is worldwide military spending, which has declined by nearly half, from 3.6 percent of gross domestic product (GDP) during the Cold War period between 1970–1990 to 1.9 percent of GDP in the period of 2010–2019.[8] Many people may not be aware that the "end of the history" narrative is a driving force behind this decline, but invisibility is one of the defining factors of a narrative that's deeply embedded.

The term "cultural embeddedness" can feel a bit abstract, and it might be challenging to categorize narratives based solely on this term. Fortunately, narrative researchers Kate C. McLean, Professor of Psychology at Western Washington University, and Moin Syed, Professor of Psychology at the University of Minnesota, have defined five key principles of master narratives. These principles can be used to evaluate how deeply a narrative is embedded in the culture and identity of a group of people:[9]

1. **Utility:** Master narratives provide a point of view about the history, goals, values, or identities of a group. This provides guidance about how to live appropriately and how to belong.
2. **Ubiquity:** For master narratives to work they must be ubiquitously shared by a group of people with a shared culture. Social norms are no longer effective (or even norms in general) if they are not broadly shared.
3. **Invisibility:** Ubiquity contributes to the third principle, which is the invisibility of master narratives. Since they are deeply embedded, they are hard for the majority to see.

4. **Compulsory Nature:** Master narratives are not neutral and have a moral component — an ideological message — which tells us how we are supposed to behave and how we are supposed to feel.
5. **Rigidity:** Master narratives get their strength and their authority from their staying power. They can be changed but it will take longer periods of time or extreme events to make that happen.

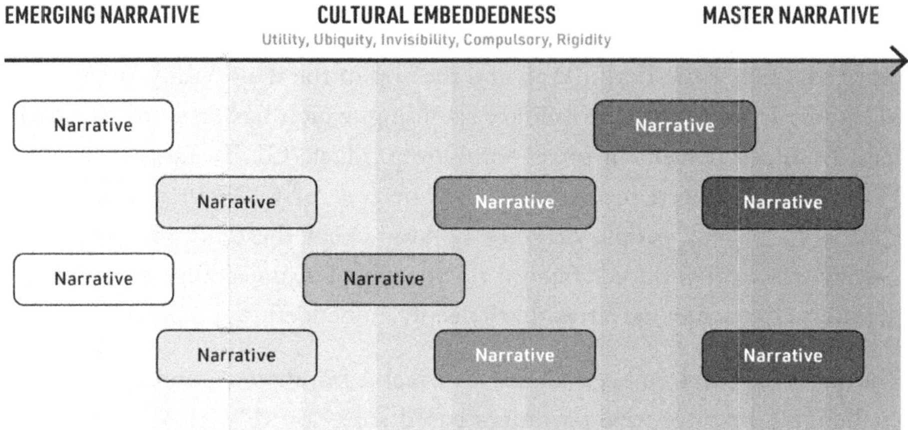

The more a narrative aligns with these five principles, the more likely it is to be a master narrative. These types of narratives are incredibly important for shaping our view of the world. They create our cultural lens and influence how we think about past, present, and future events. Let's take a deeper look at master narratives, and the various forms they take.

MASTER NARRATIVES – THE INVISIBLE FORCE

> *There are these two young fish swimming along, and they happen to meet an older fish swimming the other way, who nods at them and says, "Morning, boys. How's the water?" And the two young fish swim on for a bit, and then eventually one of them looks over at the other and goes, "What the hell is water?"*

This parable is the beginning of writer David Foster Wallace's 2005 speech to the graduating class of Kenyon College, one of the most famous commencement speeches of all time. Entitled "This Is Water," his speech reveals how the most obvious, important realities are often the ones that are the hardest to see and acknowledge.[10] This is also a key defining element of master narratives. While emerging narratives are often publicly discussed and recognizable, master narratives are a powerful invisible force that remains in the shadows but still pulls the strings.

McLean and Syed define master narratives as culturally shared stories that provide guidance for how to be a "good" member of a culture and how to live a good life. In addition to the aforementioned five principles, they also identified three basic types of master narratives:

1. Those centered on biography or lifetimes
2. Those centered on structure or sequences
3. Those that concern specific episodes or events

Biographical Master Narratives are concerned with how life should unfold and what a good life looks like. From the moment we learn our first words, we absorb thousands of stories that teach us how to live and act in the world. Some of these events and their ordering may include graduating from college, finding a job, getting married, and having a child.

I grew up in East Germany during the Cold War, a time when a minimum of 18 months military service was mandatory for all men. As a boy, I heard countless grueling stories about this phase in life which, for many, marked the end of their childhood. Eighteen-year-olds would disappear for months into barracks, and facing despotism, violence, and total subjugation, would return changed. This narrative of unchecked power and cruelty loomed large for me as I anticipated my enrollment. But then in 1989, the Wall fell. Not only did that change everyday life as I knew it, it also meant that my mandatory military service was fulfilled with the armed forces of the reunited Germany, which turned out to be a much better experience compared to what would have awaited me in East Germany. Just two decades later, in 2011, mandatory military service in Germany was suspended altogether. The military was no longer a top priority, and the end of history narrative was a major contributor to that change. Now, a new generation of young men is growing up for whom mandatory military service has entirely disappeared from their biographical master narratives.

The second type of narratives are **Structural Master Narratives**, which focus on how stories should be sequenced and played out. For instance, the narrative of redemption, which moves from negative to positive, from tragedy to triumph, is deeply embedded in US culture. The hero struggles at first, makes mistakes, and sometimes takes some wrong turns, but with hard work, luck, and learning, finally achieves success. This structure is so deeply ingrained, that you may even ask if there is any other way to tell a hero story. Here cultural differences provide many alternatives. One great example is provided by the work of Dutch social psychologist Geert Hofstede.[11]

Hofstede's research on key cultural dimensions across countries was conducted in the late 1960s and early 1970s. These cultural dimensions are presented as spectrums ranging from 1 to 120 and countries are placed on these spectrums based on their scores. One of the six dimensions is the Uncertainty Avoidance Index (UAI) which describes a society's tolerance for ambiguity. High UAI societies maintain rigid codes of belief and behavior and are less tolerant of unconventional or unpredictable people and ideas. Low UAI societies are more accepting of ambiguity and change.

The Uncertainty Avoidance Index can be seen as a gauge for how people are expected to behave when facing a problem or a challenging situation.[12] If we compare for example the data from three countries — the United States, Germany, and Japan — we see clear differences. The United States has a comparably low score of 46, as there is a fair degree of acceptance for new ideas and innovative products and a willingness to try something new or different. Failure is seen as a natural part of a process that includes failing early and often in order to learn as fast as possible.

Germany scores higher at 65 as it has a preference for systematic planning down to the details in order to create certainty that a topic or project is well thought out. The biography of a German entrepreneur like Ferdinand Porsche is an example of a hero story that is very much focused on technical expertise and hard work to overcome challenges and create engineering masterpieces.

With a score of 92, Japan is one of the most uncertainty-avoidance countries on earth. This is often attributed to the fact that the island nation is constantly threatened by natural disasters, including earthquakes, tsunamis, typhoons, and volcanic eruptions. Under these circumstances, the Japanese learned to prepare themselves for any and all potential situations. This goes not only for their emergency plans and precautions for sudden natural disasters but touches every other aspect of Japanese society. This high need for uncertainty avoidance is one of the main reasons why change is so difficult to realize in Japan.

Most cultures love stories about heroes overcoming problems, but how a hero succeeds can be very different. A company's founding story in Japan might therefore be told very differently to a similar story in the US in order to align and connect well to the established structural master narratives.

Another eye-opening example of the power of master narratives and deeply rooted, invisible cultural differences is the Brexit discussion. One could argue that the biographical master narratives of the UK are very similar to those found in the rest of Europe, especially in larger countries such as France, Germany, Poland, or Italy. What happens when we look into the UAI and try to understand the structural master narratives associated with those cultural differences? The UAI of the UK is very low, at 35 points, whereas France, for instance, is on the other side of the spectrum with 86. According to Hofstede:

> As a low UAI country the British are comfortable in ambiguous situations — the term "muddling through" is a very British way of expressing this. There are generally not too many rules in British society, but those that are there are adhered to. In work terms this results in planning that is not detail-oriented — the end goal will be clear but the detail of how we get there will be light and the actual process fluid and flexible to the emerging and changing environment.

The classic British action hero James Bond is a great example of this approach. He knows where he needs to go and which evil empire to bring to justice, but charmingly improvises in the way he gets there. In the 1964

Bond movie *Goldfinger*, Sean Connery's Bond is strapped to a table with a laser moving towards him. With no gadgets or direct means of escape, Bond uses his wits and cool demeanor to convince Goldfinger that he knows more about the villain's plan than he actually does, leading Goldfinger to spare his life for the moment. In contrast, here is a snippet from the description of the French uncertainty avoidance dimension:

> The French don't like surprises. Structure and planning are required. Before meetings and negotiations, they like to receive all necessary information. As a consequence, the French are good in developing complex technologies and systems in a stable environment, such as in the case of nuclear power plants, rapid trains, and the aviation industry.

The difference in this approach even impacts the very foundation of the legal system. The legal system of England, Northern Ireland, Scotland, and Wales is based on common law, while the EU's legal system is based on civil law.[13] In practice, this means that in Britain, a citizen can do whatever he or she wants unless it is expressly forbidden, but in Europe, a citizen can only do something if the law expressly permits it. The unbridled anger of Brexiteers on the supposedly overregulated EU bureaucracy can now be understood as the inevitable clash of two very different cultures and master narratives.

Episodic Master Narratives are specific, episodic stories about past events that are told with great frequency and in relatively the same manner. The fall of the Berlin Wall, 9/11, the nuclear disasters in Chernobyl and Fukushima, Brexit, Hurricane Katrina, and the Arab Spring are all examples of incisive events that created shared experiences and collective memories.

Returning to the example of the SVB bank run, this triggered another episodic master narrative for many: The Great Depression. During this time, desperate bank customers queued in the streets, anxiously attempting to retrieve their money amidst widespread financial collapse. The pictures from this era depict distress, panic, and the palpable fear that characterized those tumultuous years. Nobel Prize-winner Robert J. Shiller delves deep into this topic in his book, *Narrative Economics*. He discusses the enduring impact of the Great Depression's narrative, because the story of financial ruin is still something that scares people today.

Shiller notes, "The narrative of the Great Depression has been a long-lasting epidemic that outlasted the Depression itself by many decades."[14] His research reveals a fascinating trend. Interest in the story of the Great Depression has only intensified over the years. He found that there was more attention paid to the Great Depression in 2009 — following the 2008 financial crisis — than during the Great Depression itself.

Before we look into global examples of master narratives, there is also a critical view that needs to be discussed. Master narratives help legitimize the power and position of dominant groups by portraying their control as natural, inevitable, or historically justified.[15] By weaving stories that prioritize the experiences and values of the powerful, these narratives can underplay or even exclude alternative perspectives.

Master narratives often determine which events are remembered, celebrated, or forgotten and how they are interpreted. By doing so, they shape collective memory and influence historical interpretations in ways that sustain the status quo. That's why organizations like the Narrative Initiative are working to deepen knowledge about narratives and their instrumental role in social change.[16] Narratives define what we imagine is possible and whether we feel we have the power to achieve those possibilities. In that sense, changes can only move at the speed at which narratives develop and change.

For example, the structural master narrative of redemption focuses heavily on the concept of "pulling yourself up by your bootstraps" as critical to overcoming adversity, without acknowledging the structural disadvantages faced by underprivileged groups.

GLOBAL MASTER NARRATIVES

Whenever I talk about the power of master narratives, the question of whether there's a list of important ones comes up often. Unfortunately, there is not. Master narratives, by definition, are rarely openly visible from the outside and even difficult to recognize by insiders. The three basic types of master narratives we've discussed are a good starting point for thinking about them more systematically in a given communication case.

Siberia
Uchi-Soto
Bali Bali
Chinese Dream
The Asian
Century
Karma
Face Culture
Rojak
Mateship
Tall Poppy Syndrome
Māori

Nevertheless, I have collected a few master narratives from various global regions and countries to provide inspiration and motivation to dig deeper. An important disclaimer for this list is that it is a highly subjective view, and the goal in providing these master narratives is not to make a value judgment. They are only a tiny fraction of the prevailing narratives. Master narratives could also be distinguished between how outsiders look at a region and what people or nations believe about themselves. This map intends to focus on the latter.

Siberia, known for its punishing climate and remote expanses, carries a narrative deeply intertwined with stories of banishment, punishment, and survival.

The Chinese Dream, embraced by Xi Jinping in 2013, emphasizes the collective strength of the Chinese people.

The Asian Century refers to the belief that Asian countries will dominate the 21st century in terms of economic growth, political influence, and cultural impact.

Bali Bali, in English hurry hurry, is a South Korean working mentality characterized by a sense of urgency and haste.

Face Culture plays an important role in many Asian countries and encompasses the fear of social disapproval among individuals or groups, impacting interpersonal relationships and emphasizing social harmony.

Uchi-Soto is a Japanese cultural distinction between Uchi, the inner circle where genuine feelings are expressed, and Soto, the outer circle where social norms guide public interactions.

Karma is a master narrative in India and describes the cumulative actions of an individual across present and past lives, shaping their destiny in future existences.

Rojak, meaning "mixed" in Malay, is a traditional dish with varying ingredients in India, China, and Malaysia, symbolizing the cultural blend of Singapore.

Mateship, deeply rooted in the value of equality, embodies friendship, shared bonds, or a collective ethos, particularly evident in Australian culture.

Tall-Poppy-Syndrome describes the avoidance of excessive boasting driven by the fear of backlash, especially among close friends and family in countries like Australia, New Zealand, and the United Kingdom.

Māori, New Zealand's indigenous people, continue to shape the country's identity despite strong Westernization.

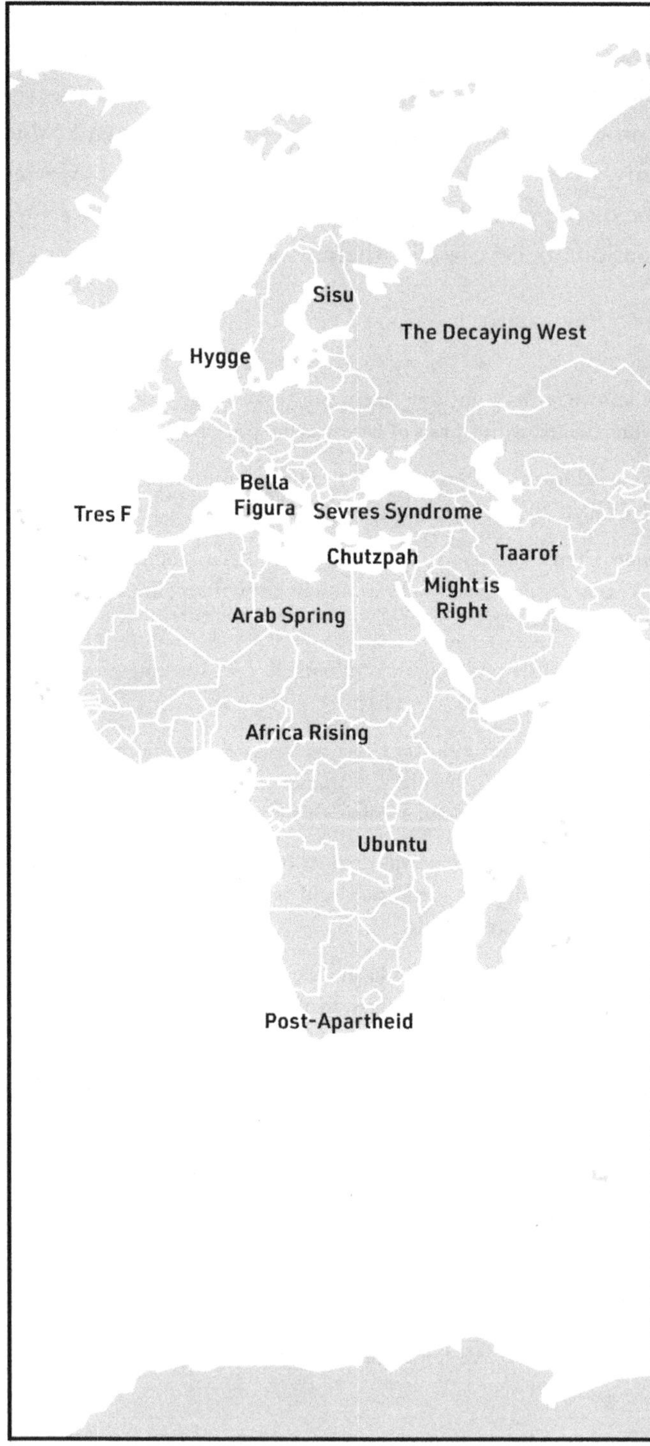
Sisu
The Decaying West
Hygge
Bella
Figura
Tres F
Sevres Syndrome
Chutzpah
Taarof
Might is
Right
Arab Spring
Africa Rising
Ubuntu
Post-Apartheid

Sisu (Finnish for "inner") describes an individual's ability to persevere through life's most daunting challenges, rooted in a resilient and courageous mentality.

Hygge represents a Danish mentality focused on cultivating a cozy atmosphere and cherishing meaningful moments with friends and family.

The Decaying West is a long-established Russian narrative implying the decline of Western countries and their principles, often cited to promote the superiority of Russia's traditional values.

Tres F, symbolizing Fado (a melancholic chant), Football, and Fatima (a pilgrimage site), was an ideology embraced by former Portuguese dictator Salazar to appease the people.

Bella Figura is an Italian concept emphasizing polished public appearance but also encompasses behavior, communication, and etiquette.

Sevres Syndrome is a Turkish theory asserting that Western powers are strategically encircling the nation with the intent to partition it.

Chutzpah embodies a bold and fearless attitude that can be perceived as arrogant, yet it's simultaneously respected for its confidence and is most closely associated with Jewish culture.

Might is Right is a philosophy that suggests power and strength are the ultimate arbiters of what is just and right and is not tied to a single country but can be found in many cultures worldwide.

Taarof, a cultural tradition in Iran, involves a verbal dance of polite gestures and pleasantries during various interactions, occasionally without genuine feeling.

The Arab Spring signifies a wave of democratic movements and political reform across North-African/Arab nations in the 2010s, driven by a quest for human rights and an end to authoritarian regimes.

Africa Rising is a narrative coined in the early 2000s to depict Sub-Saharan Africa's substantial economic growth.

Ubuntu is an African philosophy that encapsulates the belief that our wellbeing is intertwined with the wellbeing of others, reflecting shared responsibility and interconnectedness.

Post-Apartheid refers to the era after the termination of apartheid in South Africa, showcasing the empowerment of people of color amidst persisting problems like racial inequality, poverty, and unemployment.

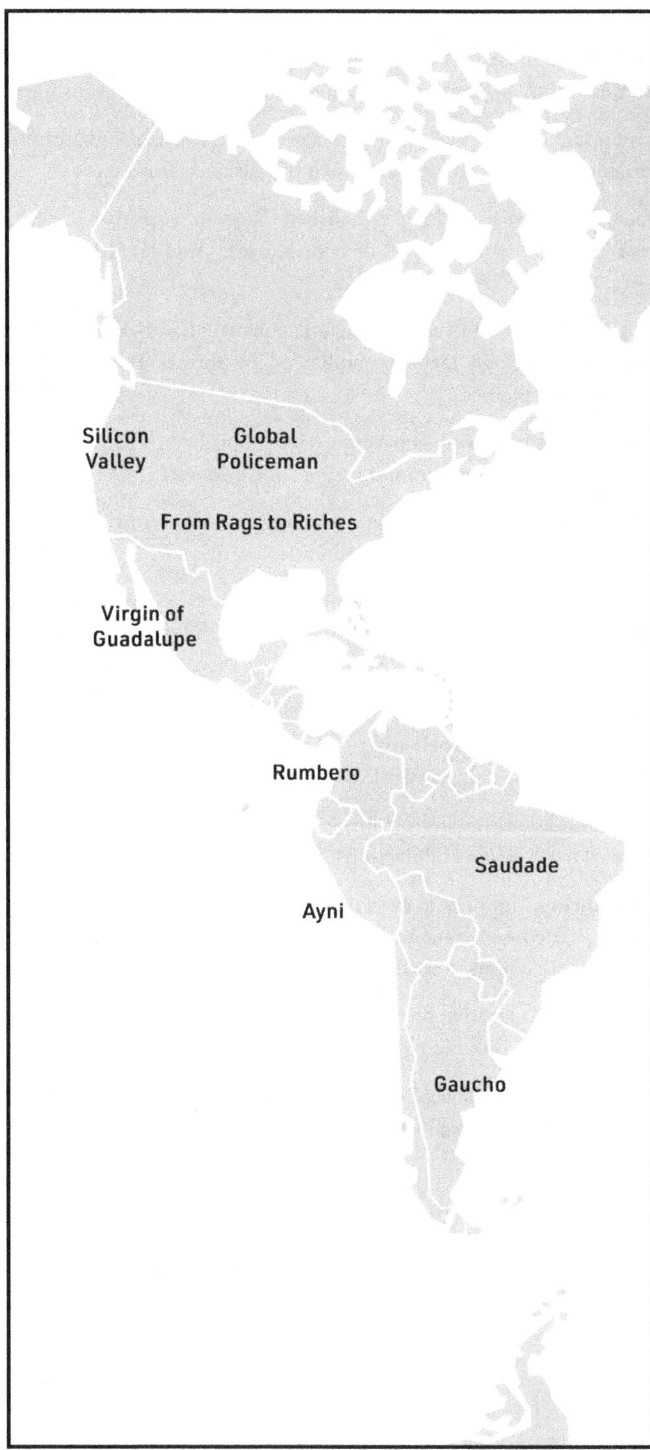
Silicon Valley
Global Policeman
From Rags to Riches
Virgin of Guadalupe
Rumbero
Saudade
Ayni
Gaucho

Global Policeman is a designation assigned to the US after World War II, emphasizing its taken-for-granted role in intervening in international conflicts.

Silicon Valley, the global epicenter of technology entrepreneurship, is where disruption prevails, diverse minds converge, and the American Dream thrives.

From Rags to Riches is a deeply ingrained cultural story that underscores the American Dream. Anyone, regardless of their background, can achieve significant success through hard work, determination, and perseverance.

The Virgin of Guadalupe, stemming from a Mexican narrative in 1531, refers to the Virgin Mary, mother of Jesus. She played a pivotal role in Mexico's fight for independence — uniting indigenous beliefs with Catholicism — and has evolved into a powerful symbol of unity, cultural identity, and faith.

Rumbero vividly captures the Colombian spirit of living a well balanced life and embodies the "work hard, play hard" ethos.

Ayni, a Quechua term translating to "today for you, tomorrow for me," symbolizes reciprocity and mutual support within the Andean community.

Saudade is closely connected to Portuguese culture and language and describes a deep feeling caused by a melancholic or nostalgic longing for something or someone that is absent or has been lost.

Gaucho, in Argentina, embodies a skilled horseman of mixed European and Indigenous descent, exemplifying values of independence, pride, tradition, and the diverse cultural heritage of the nation.

EXPANDING THE NARRATIVE LANDSCAPE

So far, we have examined the narrative landscape through the lens of how deeply narratives are embedded in the culture and identity of a group.

For a homogeneous audience, these emerging and master narratives might already be a good description of their narrative landscape. However, in many cases, an audience is not homogeneous. An international company with locations in various countries that communicates with customers or employees will face a much broader narrative landscape. Some emerging and master narratives are shared between all stakeholders, while many other narratives are only known and important on the local level. With this in mind, we introduce a second dimension to the narrative landscape, which delves into the distribution of narratives — in other words, how widespread are narratives?

Imagine a pilot flying for the Dutch airline KLM and living in De Pijp, a trendy neighborhood in Amsterdam. She would know **local narratives** from the neighborhood, narratives from Amsterdam, and narratives from the Netherlands and Europe. She would also be aware of local narratives from her profession as a pilot, as well as those from her employer KLM. Add narratives from her family, friends, places to which she regularly flies, and so on. If she talks to another mother at her son's school, she can assume common knowledge of the local school narratives. If she talks to a fellow KLM pilot, she can assume a common understanding of shared narratives about flying and KLM. In contrast, if she talks to an outsider about her work in the cockpit, there will be fewer shared narratives, and she will need to do more explaining. Whenever we communicate, we naturally take the narrative landscape into account and ideally adapt our communication.

The term "local" here is meant in the broadest sense because any attribute might create these narratives. Members of a family might have their own local narratives, as might inhabitants of a city or country or professionals like pilots or teachers.

Local narratives can also become deeply embedded and create a **local identity.** From a young age, we are exposed to narratives — stories from family, cultural tales, national histories, and media accounts — that influence our understanding of who we are. These stories provide a framework for understanding oneself in relation to others and the world and creating a personal identity. Identity is defined as a subjective, constructed, and evolving story of how one came to be the person one currently is. This story aims to integrate the past, present, and future in order to create a sense of personal continuity.[17] The creation of our identity is very much impacted by the narrative landscape that surrounds us.

Organizations also have an identity that is shaped by the history, culture, leadership vision, and shared experiences of its members. This collective sense of self can evolve as the organization grows or adapts to changes in its environment.

Founding stories and insights from "the early days" often create local identity at organizations. Take the Amazon "door desk" as an example. In Amazon's early days, CEO Jeff Bezos looked at desks for sale at Home Depot and realized that doors were much cheaper, so he decided to buy a door and put some legs on it.[18] With that, the Amazon "door desk" was born. The scrappy, do-it-yourself desk turned into one of Amazon's most distinctive symbols of the culture of being focused on efficiency and cost reduction. More than 20 years later, thousands of Amazon employees worldwide still work each day on modern versions of those original door desks.

Narrative researchers Michael Müller and Christine Erlach emphasize how important an organization's history is for understanding its present identity and its ability to craft a powerful picture of the future. They observe that often, companies dismiss the past with a reluctant "Let the past rest; we want to look to the future." However, they argue that such an attitude is shortsighted. Knowing the stories of "how we became what we are today" means understanding the current culture, including aspects that may not be immediately visible. Developing an organization for the future starts with the present. The past is the only source of information available to the company to narrate its identity or to learn about itself from external narratives. Without an identity, mastering the present or looking to the future is impossible.[19]

The two dimensions — cultural embeddedness and distribution — create a space for the narrative landscape populated with countless narratives. As a rough simplification, we can use a diagram to divide the space into four quadrants to approximate the types of narratives we can expect in these areas.

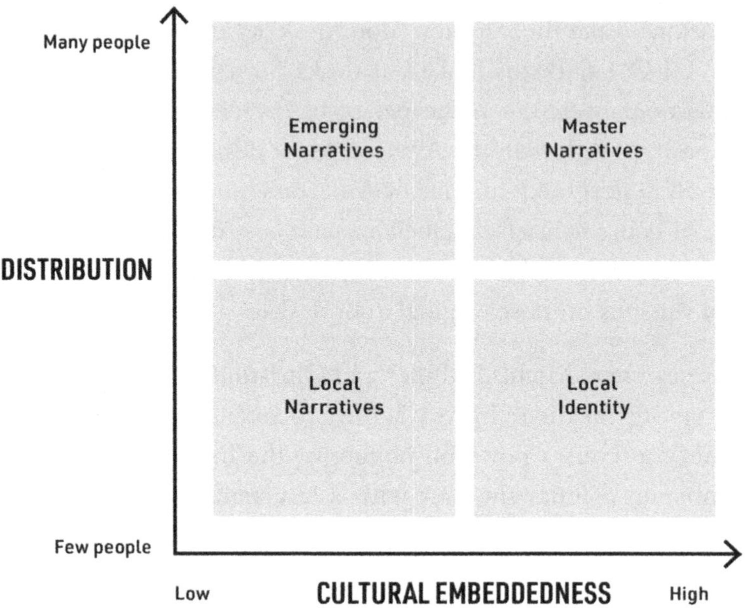

It's important to keep in mind that the goal of a narrative landscape is not to determine a narrative's validity by its specific placement on the map; it's a mental model to think about the impact of the narratives at hand and the role they play for the audience:

- **Master narratives** are deeply embedded in the collective mind of a large group of people.
- **Emerging narratives** revolve around new or more recent events and are well-known to a broad, sometimes even global, audience.
- **Local narratives** are equally current on the time axis, but their distribution will be more limited to specific groups of people. The most extreme form of a local narrative could be a personal narrative that only exists in the mind of a single person.
- **Local identity** is created through deeply embedded narratives for individuals or groups.

HOW TO CREATE A NARRATIVE MAP

One could try to build a narrative map with all the narratives out there. But besides being an impossible task, it would not be very helpful. It would have too much noise and too many contrary narratives to be of any use for a communications strategy.

It's much more useful to think in terms of specific situations: a company needs to communicate a major change to its employees. The launch of a product into a new market. A response to a crisis situation. The strategy for a political campaign. Remember the initial focus groups of the Brexit Leave campaigns and the resulting strategy document? At its core was an analysis of the narrative landscape, which was a major factor in shaping the Leave campaign.

Creating a narrative map is most effective when considering the existing narratives of an audience you seek to address for a specific purpose. Don't worry about defining everything in one session. A narrative map is a tool that can evolve, be revisited, and be edited multiple times.

There are various perspectives from which stories and narratives about an organization or a subject can be told. A good map will attempt to make these different narrative voices visible. Don't be concerned if perspectives create dissonance and contradictions. It's not about achieving harmony. Rather, it's about embracing versatility.

Organizations aiming to undertake a narrative mapping exercise should seek to collect:

- **Stories/narratives from us:** What does the organization say about itself? This might be founding stories or stories about leaders, changes, or current challenges. This specifically includes all perspectives from the past, the present, and the future.
- **Stories/narratives about us:** What are others saying about us? This might include customers, investors, the press, or discussions on social media.

- **Related cultural stories/narratives:** Which current events or topics are potentially relevant to our subject? Which major trends will likely come our way? What is being said about our industry?
- **Black holes:** Which stories or narratives are potentially controversial and might have a negative impact on our message?
- **Master narratives:** Which biographical, structural, or episodic master narratives can be identified to support or oppose our message?
- **Local narratives and identity:** Who are our key stakeholder groups and are there specific topics they care about?

These categories are not sharply defined. Much of what you find could fall into several categories. But that doesn't matter. On the contrary, such surprises can be insightful: Do stories about your organization contradict each other, or are they aligned? What are the discrepancies, and what can you learn from them about your narrative strategy?[20]

Here is an example of a narrative map for a defense startup like Anduril:

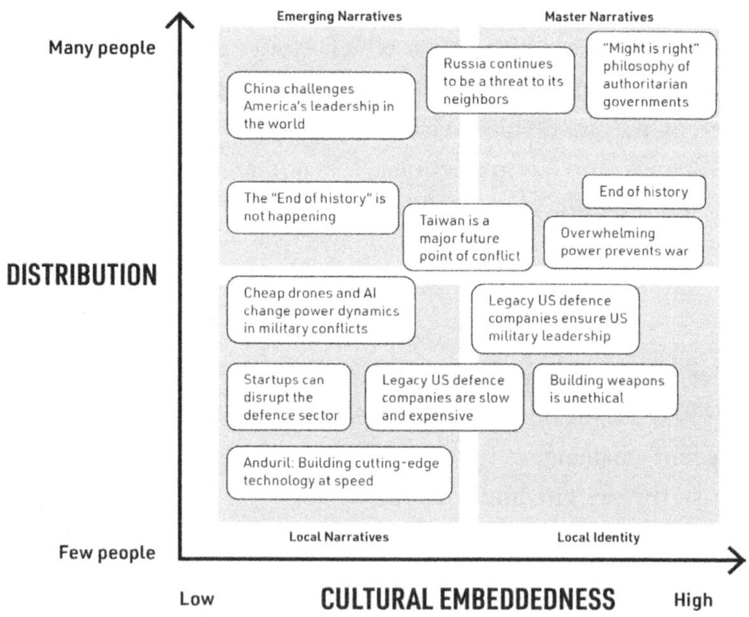

A narrative map for Anduril and defense technologies

There could be many more narratives, and this map could be more targeted toward a specific audience, such as potential investors, customers, or the general public. The structure aids in considering existing narratives and sharing these insights with a team. The more a new narrative and its stories integrate with this existing narrative landscape, the greater the resonance will be.

One insight from this particular map could be that agreeing on the need for weapons is challenging when people believe in fundamentally opposing master narratives or are not fully aware of their counterparts' cultural lenses. For instance, the "might is right" narrative is less prevalent in Western cultures but deeply embedded in many authoritarian societies worldwide. Gad Saad, a behavioral scientist, writes: "In the Middle East, the 'might is right' maxim is operative throughout every element of society. It is a deeply hierarchical society wherein all dyadic relationships are viewed through the prism of established dominance relationships. Hence, many of the Western values that we construe as noble are viewed as manifestations of weakness. It is truly extraordinary the extent to which Western leaders have zero understanding of these deep cultural differences."[21]

Effective communicators need to be aware of the cultural lens, meaning the narrative landscape of their audience, as this is the only way to truly establish common narratives that align and unite the different viewpoints of people, groups, and societies. While we have spent some time exploring the foundations of narrative creation and landscape mapping, it's time to turn to a highly practical and somewhat controversial topic — changing existing narratives. For this, we will examine another startup that is challenging an existing industry and its narrative landscape.

4. HOW TO SHIFT A NARRATIVE

THE PLANT-BASED MEAT BATTLE

On the day it debuted in May 2019, Beyond Meat's stock skyrocketed by 163 percent, marking a major American company's most impressive one-day surge in almost 20 years. The company stood at the forefront of a protein revolution that brought a touch of Silicon Valley to the once-niche market of meat alternatives. Sales of plant-based meat surged 74 percent between 2018 and 2021, propelled by both savvy marketing campaigns and growing concerns over the environmental footprint of traditional meat production. Experts like Barclays forecasted the market would reach $140 billion USD by 2030.[1]

Only a few years later, things no longer looked so bright. By late 2023, Beyond Meat had lost more than 90 percent of its valuation compared to its early days in the stock market. The company was struggling to deliver the growth that everyone was expecting. Customers were trying the products but not adopting their consumption as a new habit at scale. To address the issue of recurring purchases, the company began working on a fourth version of its imitation beef burger while also releasing a thinner version with a new formula and texture.

While product quality and likeability are important, a significant albeit less apparent part of the struggle is an ongoing narrative battle about the benefits and challenges of plant-based meat. Beyond Meat and others initially positioned their products as high-tech food. Their burgers, while made entirely from plants, imitated beef so closely they even mimicked the bleed of meat by using beetroot juice.[2] The other key message was around sustainability. With plant-based burgers, consumers would help to fight climate change and reduce the 15 percent of global greenhouse emissions from livestock farming.[3]

The high-tech narrative made it easy for traditional market players, such as existing meat producers, to portray plant-based food as highly processed and potentially unhealthy. The Center for Consumer Freedom, an organization campaigning on behalf of the meat industry, has run full-page ads in national newspapers in the US, attacking plant-based companies for their processing methods. One campaign compared plant-based meat to dog food, while another labeled them "ultra-processed imitations that are assembled in industrial factories."[4]

These campaigns seemed to impact customer perception as industry research indicates that the percentage of people who thought plant-based meats were healthy was in decline. Beyond Meat CEO Ethan Brown said in the company's Q2 earnings call in August 2023:

> In the two-year period 2020 to 2022, the percentage of US consumers who believe plant-based meats are healthy dropped from 50 percent to 38 percent, according to the Food Marketing Institute. As was the case during the ascent of plant-based milk, this change in perception is not without encouragement from interest groups who have succeeded in seeding doubt and fear around the ingredients and process used to create our and other plant-based meats.[5]

Beyond Meat labeled these campaigns as misinformation and has since been trying to take back the narrative. It launched a campaign called "There is Goodness Here" that focuses on sharing and celebrating the farming origins of their ingredients and delineated clean and simple steps taken to produce plant-based meats. A second activity they've undertaken involves building a body of research about the health benefits of their products. This includes the certification of plant-based meat "Beyond Steak" as a heart-healthy food by the American Heart Association.

The case of Beyond Meat and the plant meat industry provides fascinating insights into the mechanics of narrative change. We are witnessing a significant narrative battle, with meat lobby groups challenging the initial offerings of plant meat producers. Now, there are campaigns addressing these accusations.

Let's look at the narrative map for plant-based meat. It's a simplified example, as there could be many more narratives, especially locally. For example, Beyond Meat is sold in more than 80 countries worldwide, and perceptions about eating vegetarian differ greatly in many countries. Over 1.5 billion people worldwide do not eat meat. However, more than 95 percent of them would eat meat if they could afford it.[6] The current narrative battle is centered around the health effects of plant-based meat. Even though this is a more recent discussion, it is so powerful because it is connected to powerful master narratives around personal health and well-being.

Regarding narrative change, the first challenge was to present an alternative narrative, while the current Beyond Meat campaign represents a counternarrative. Both are distinct strategies for narrative change and will be discussed in more detail in this chapter. But before delving into that, let's look at some basic mechanics of narrative change.

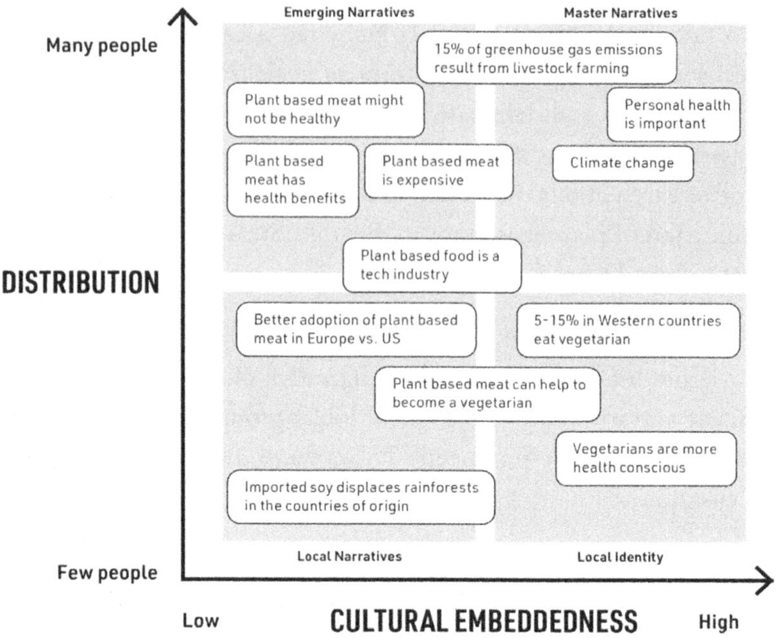

A narrative map for plant-based meat

CHANGING THE NARRATIVE LANDSCAPE

Who enjoys having their mind changed? Most of us do not. We experience discomfort or stress when new information threatens an existing belief or narrative. The theory behind this insight is cognitive dissonance, which was first posited in 1957 by Leon Festinger, an American social psychologist.[7] Cognitive dissonance theory suggests that individuals experience discomfort when they simultaneously hold two or more contradictory beliefs, values, or attitudes. If you learn something that does not fit your existing narrative landscape, you may be tempted to ignore or reframe the new information to avoid this discomfort.

For example, during the first long drive of a newly-purchased car you may discover something you do not like. This conflicts with your belief that buying this car was a good decision. Your brain struggles to reconcile the excitement and positive feelings with the new negative feelings generated by the discovery of an undesirable aspect. What do you do? You may focus on the car's positive aspects, convincing yourself that these outweigh the negatives. You may also try to change your perception of the disliked feature, perhaps by seeing it as an opportunity for customization. However, there might be a point when you have discovered so many things you dislike that you will change your mind and try to return the car.

As we have seen, not all narratives are created equal, and there are differences in their changeability. The benefit of a more nuanced understanding of the narrative landscape is to know where change can happen and where such efforts are in vain. For instance, there is little chance of success in trying to contest master narratives directly. As narrative researcher Steven Corman writes about master narratives in Afghanistan:

> It is no more feasible to convince Muslims that they have no internal and external enemies than it is to convince Americans that they live in the land of the enslaved and the home of the cowardly. In both cases, these ideas are too deeply ingrained to be disrupted, and efforts to do so would be seen as ridiculous.[8]

The most important master narratives are deeply ingrained in a culture's identity and are often seen as non-negotiable. Researchers refer to these as "sacred values," noting that individuals typically won't compromise on them, even for material gain. Sacred values such as family welfare, national loyalty, religious commitment, honor, and justice are considered absolute and inviolable.

Understanding an opponent's sacred values can facilitate resolution in difficult negotiations. Contrary to the common belief that such values should be saved for last or bypassed with material offers during a negotiation, these approaches usually backfire. Offering material gains in exchange for sacred values is often viewed as insulting and impedes resolution.

In the context of narrative change, it's vital to acknowledge that not all groups or societies are open to new ideas or values, particularly if they see these as threats to their sacred values and dominant master narratives. However, this understanding provides a way to introduce new ideas and narratives in a way that resonates with the existing narrative landscape and aligns with the audience's sacred values.[9]

Changing personal narratives resulting from an audience's direct personal experience is equally challenging. There is no way to tell panicking founders trying to get their funds out of Silicon Valley Bank that everything is fine when the banking software no longer works. Boasting great customer service will be useless if your customers are having bad experiences with your call center. The proof is in the pudding, as they say.

A change is likely achievable for local and emerging narratives that are not yet deeply ingrained. If these narratives can be altered, then as a subsequent step they could gradually influence master or personal narratives and, over a much longer timeframe, even affect identities.

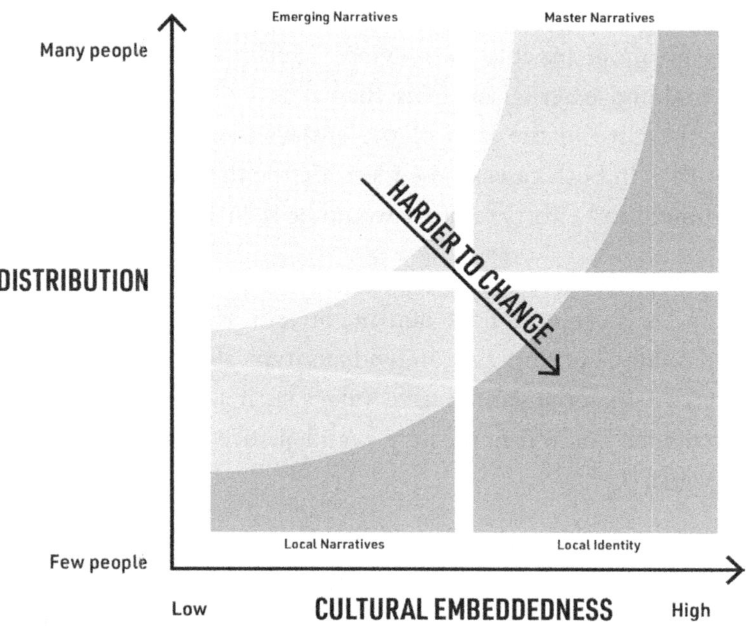

Some areas of the narrative map are much easier to change compared to others.

There are different ways to think about changing narratives. The more obvious is a head-on counternarrative attempting to challenge existing beliefs directly. The other option is an alternative narrative, offering a different perspective and focus than the dominant story. Let's look at both in more detail.

COUNTERNARRATIVES CHALLENGE EXISTING NARRATIVES HEAD-ON

In 1994, Lidl, a German supermarket chain, launched its first store in the UK. 29 years later, they've expanded to over 960 stores, challenging the dominance of the "big four" supermarkets — Tesco, Sainsbury's, Asda, and Morrisons. After initial fast growth based on a low-cost strategy, the ride started to get bumpy. Despite the fact that Lidl products in the UK were consistently rated as better quality than those of their big-name competitors, UK consumers didn't think of Lidl as a supermarket that sold quality products. Instead, it was seen as a cheap supermarket for low-income families. At that time, Lidl's brand strategy report concluded:

> Lidl's personality is not distinct from their competitor's offerings. Lidl's brand personality reflects an outdated, cheap, European, cluttered product range, which is negatively perceived by some consumers.[10]

People knew Lidl was affordable, but many didn't realize they sold quality products. This gave Lidl a chance to shift perceptions and build a counternarrative about the surprisingly good quality of their products. They emphasized that cheap doesn't mean poor quality, and that customers can save money without giving up on good products.

They launched the #LIDLsurprises campaign, which showcased a fresh brand voice, playing a key role in changing how people saw them. The campaign was playful and smart, turning Lidl's past reputation into a strength. One ad, for example, showed a small farmer's market somewhere in London with people tasting food and being surprised once they learned all of it was from Lidl. The campaign let customers admit that Lidl's products were once seen as subpar and even welcomed such frankness. Lidl also moved away from its old media approach, which relied on door drops to get across its price message. Instead, it focused on engaging with customers via social media and in stores to both attract new customers and get current ones to spend more money.

The new messaging articulated a simple but effective narrative: "Our products are surprisingly good — why not try them? And because of the price, you've pretty much got nothing to lose."[11]

Lidl changed their voice, and their image followed. They weren't just seen as a low-cost option but a real competitor to big supermarkets. The new brand voice and narrative increased their audience size on social media and elevated Lidl to "most positively discussed supermarket" on Twitter. In the first year of the new brand voice, awareness of Lidl grew by 80 percent, and over half a million more customers started shopping with them. Lidl's market share in the UK went from 4.5 percent in 2017 to 7.7 percent in 2023. At the same time, all of the "big four" competitors lost market share.[12]

The goal of a counternarrative is to create cognitive dissonance by deconstructing and discrediting existing beliefs. However, the counternarrative strategy has a potential challenge: it might reinforce the original narrative if the audience is highly engaged. The more an individual thinks about an idea, the harder it becomes to counter or displace it.[13] For instance, in experimental settings where participants were exposed to a generic counternarrative after seeing extremist propaganda, they were more likely to align with the propaganda. When people feel their freedom to hold certain views or beliefs is threatened, they might be more inclined to resist the message and strengthen their preexisting beliefs.[14]

An idea with a lot of mindshare will be more challenging to change. In regard to organizational change, this may also mean that communicators need to argue against narratives that they previously established themselves. An example of this is Rover Cars in the 1990s. Like many other companies at the time, Rover had significantly invested in employee satisfaction programs. As a result, the company had fabulously high scores for employee satisfaction and corporate pride. However, that pride contributed to employees' resistance to change because the counternarrative that change was suddenly necessary didn't fit the dominant narrative that everyone was doing a great job.[15]

Counternarratives are the first choice when an existing belief needs to be addressed and changed and cannot be left on the sidelines. Facing a crisis, Silicon Valley Bank had to counter the existing belief that this might be a bank run that could result in bankruptcy. Beyond Meat had to address health concerns and make the case that plant meat is good for your health. If narratives are harmful to an organization and they connect to powerful master narratives like financial survival or personal health, there is no other way than to address them head-on.

The same applies to Lidl, as the quality of food that we eat every day directly impacts our well-being and health. The core challenge of counter-narratives is that they must shift an existing belief system. The arguments and stories built to do that need to be extremely convincing. Lidl did this masterfully with TV ads such as the one for MSC Scottish Mussels. A social media user, Chris wrote online:

> *I worry where Lidl get their seafood. I don't want to find it's from a ditch.*

Lidl UK answered him with this message:

> *Sounds like a challenge Chris. Fancy working in our ditch?*

Lidl invited him to join a Scottish mussel fishing ship to see that the mussels are sourced from beautifully clean Scottish coastal waters on the Isle of Mull. They end up sitting on the boat, eating mussels, and Chris seems truly impressed and apologizes for the "ditch" analogy. The ad shows fundamental success factors for counternarratives. It's essential to establish a connection with your audience, acknowledge the existing belief, and then turn it around.

Chris Voss was the FBI's chief international hostage and kidnapping negotiator from 2003 to 2007 and wrote the book *Never Split the Difference* about his experiences of changing the minds of criminals. He explains a technique called mirroring:

> It's almost laughably simple: for the FBI, a "mirror" is when you repeat the last three words (or the critical one to three words) of what someone has just said. Of the entirety of the FBI's hostage negotiation skill set, mirroring is the closest one gets to a Jedi mind trick. Simple, and yet uncannily effective. By repeating back what people say, you trigger this mirroring instinct and your counterpart will inevitably elaborate on what was just said and sustain the process of connecting.[16]

Mirroring demonstrates empathy. A 2022 Stanford University study proved the power of empathy in political conversations, particularly around the topic of gun control laws. Participants were asked to read arguments about the benefits of empathy and then write messages to someone from an opposing political party. Those who were exposed to the "high value" of empathy were almost twice as inclined to use understanding and unifying language, such as "we all want" or "I understand that." Instead of diving into controversial issues directly, they spoke of shared objectives like safety and referenced respected foundations such as the US Constitution. Readers from the opposite political spectrum found these empathetic writers more likable and persuasive and were even likely to soften their stance on gun control laws after reading their messages.[17]

Understanding counternarratives and using them effectively involves integrating them into the existing narrative landscape and presenting them empathetically. However, in a polarized world, it's increasingly challenging to penetrate echo chambers with opposing opinions. Audiences tend to ignore counterarguments to their existing beliefs, seeking confirmation elsewhere. In this case, an effective tool for bridging gaps can be alternative narratives. These do not directly confront existing beliefs but instead opt for a subtler approach, which can be highly effective and powerful in changing the hearts and minds of an audience.

ALTERNATIVE NARRATIVES LEAD WITH SHARED VALUES

> *How do you fight an idea? With another idea.*
>
> — From the movie *Ben-Hur*

Australia Day on January 26 is the official national day that marks the first landing of a British fleet on the island. For the average Australian, it's a summer holiday for barbecues and beers with friends. For Aboriginal communities, it marks invasion and the onset of genocide. There is a significant movement advocating for changing the date of Australia Day to a day that is more inclusive and respectful of Australia's indigenous peoples. However, only about one-third of Australians currently support this initiative.[18] Language is important, and this showed when it came to the sentiment around Australia Day. The stories that sought to get indigenous perspectives often painted a picture of pain and suffering, depicting the day as very difficult for the Aboriginal and Torres Strait Islander people.

The narrative would be one of "deficit messaging" as most stories about Aboriginal communities and Torres Strait Islanders come from outside entities such as the government or corporations. They have the valid intent to support First Nations people but focus on what is lacking or problematic. This type of messaging emphasizes shortcomings rather than strengths or potential solutions. For Australia Day, indigenous people are usually interviewed, but the story would be *about* them and their pain, not *from* them.

Kelly Williams, an indigenous Bundjalung woman, works at the Australian Broadcasting Company and pushed to establish an alternative narrative about First Nations and Australia Day. Her goal was to reframe the message from one of deficit to that of justice and self-determination. She explains how she changed the coverage for Australia Day: "When I was actually leading that coverage, I changed those headlines to celebrating indigenous culture, and that for me was the pivot moment putting us in that leadership frame and celebrating the resilience and survival of Aboriginal culture in Australia."[19]

The dominant narrative regarding Australia Day and First Nations people was that it was a difficult day for them. A counternarrative would not have worked in this case because, after all, that dominant narrative was true. The alternative narrative, to celebrate resilience and survival, is powerful because it still recognized the issue but also looked forward and created something to be proud of.

Alternative narratives provide a different perspective or interpretation of events or ideas than the dominant story. Unlike counternarratives, they don't necessarily exist to resist or challenge the dominant narrative directly; they simply offer a different take or focus. In short, they present alternative ideas that are supported and encouraged.

Instead of leading off with problems, new narratives that first link to shared master narratives have proven much more effective at shifting opinions.

Australia Day, like most other national days, is a master narrative. By accepting this day as one to celebrate, the messaging of celebrating resilience and survival was much better connected to the narrative landscape of all Australians. A similar example is the discussion in many progressive countries about equality for same-sex marriages. The messaging became much more successful once people made the debate about the values of commitment and family, which are broadly shared and understood master narratives even for very conservative audiences.[20]

Another excellent example of an alternative narrative comes from the city of Berlin in the 2000s. In those euphoric years right after the Wall fell in 1989, things weren't looking so good for the reunited capital of Germany. The city suffered under a high financial burden but lacked the resources to properly fund necessary developments. The former West Berlin was never an economic powerhouse due to its isolation from the rest of West Germany, and most businesses from East Berlin were unable to survive in the newly entered free market. The unemployment rate in 2005 was 19 percent.[21] Berlin had an image of being chaotic, poor, and badly governed. Other German states had to transfer money to the capital and complained about it being a financial black hole.

On the bright side, despite being poor, Berlin had a reputation for excitement. During the divided era, West Berlin had some special rules: young male residents were exempt from military service, and clubs could stay open without a curfew. This reputation drew a unique set of people to Berlin, including cultural icons like David Bowie and Iggy Pop. The city became even more diverse after the Wall came down. Unlike in most other Western capital cities, people didn't need much money to live and experience a lot. Rent was still cheap, and the open spaces and wastelands in the cityscape had yet to be filled. Flourishing was not synonymous with beauty but with the fact that anything and everything seemed possible.

In 2003, Berlin mayor Klaus Wowereit started to coin a claim that became a powerful narrative over the years: "Berlin is poor but sexy." This was not a counternarrative to the accusation of being dysfunctional and squandering other people's money. It instead created a different focus that acknowledged the city's challenges but simultaneously painted a powerful picture of breaking from the traditional norms of what a prosperous capital city should be all about.

A supporting aspect that could even be seen as part of a developing narrative constellation was Wowereit publically coming out as gay. It contributed to his image as a progressive and modern leader, aligning with the image of Berlin he later portrayed. Berlin, known for its liberal and inclusive atmosphere, was fittingly led by someone who was openly part of the LGBTQ+ community, a rarity in high political office at the time. This alternative narrative proved magnetic, attracting people from around the world. In 2011, *the Hollywood Reporter* published an article entitled "How Berlin Became the Coolest City on the Planet."[22]

As a result, startups and the creative industry have seen phenomenal growth in Berlin while the city is fast approaching four million inhabitants. Unfortunately, as has been the case in many other fast-growing cities, gentrification of many inner-city neighborhoods gained momentum. "Poor" is no longer an apt description for Berlin. But in part, it's the narrative of poor and sexy that brought an influx of people and culture to an otherwise dysfunctional and underfunded city. The narrative drove action.

IDEAS FOR ACTION

Developing and changing a narrative map is not an exact science. It is not comparable to the laws of physics or mathematical calculations. However, the methods and approaches are very helpful for structuring, understanding, and deriving possible strategies in complex narrative situations. It is not about completeness or ultimate accuracy; it is about understanding the narrative landscape better and being able to place one's own narratives more consciously in context. Here are some more ideas on how to achieve that.

Lead with shared values, not problems: Start with what we all believe in, not the issues. Most of the time, people talk about the problems first, then solutions, before finally asking for action. But people already have enough problems of their own and don't want to hear more. It's natural to want to talk about the big issues affecting us, but this doesn't always grab attention.

Instead, if we begin by talking about common beliefs and values, people are more likely to support new ideas or changes.

This approach is valid for both counternarratives and alternative narratives. We have discussed how the Lidl ad acknowledged the perception of low-quality products and then moved to a solution. The same approach can be applied to explain and justify a change program inside an organization. Start with the values that the organization stands for and the future everyone is working towards. Any change should be grounded in these shared values and shared identity.

Is it actually a change? Marketer Seth Godin argues that the most successful marketing strategies are trying to connect a story with an audience's existing worldview. People do not want to change; instead, they want to have their worldview reinforced:

> Great stories agree with our worldview. The best stories don't teach people anything new. Instead, the best stories agree with what the audience already believes and make the members of the audience feel smart and secure when reminded how right they were in the first place.[23]

A program to increase efficiency at a company can be positioned as a change that's needed because of economic headwinds or rising internal costs. But it's also possible to connect this efficiency campaign to the roots and early days of the company, where efficiency always played a big role and was actually the key reason that an organization was able to grow and be successful in the first place. In this case, the positioning is not that of change but of reconnecting to the original value and identity of the company.

Choose your words carefully: Counternarratives and alternative narratives refer to stories or interpretations that differ from a dominant or mainstream narrative. Both have in common that they will only work if they fit the existing narrative landscape of the audience. This means choosing the correct narratives with which to connect and avoiding the wrong ones. As master narratives are often brought to life with a single word, words absolutely do matter.

Use the future to change the present: It's sometimes hard to deconstruct existing narratives and look for deeper connected narratives. Sohail Inayatullah, a Pakistani-Australian futurist, has developed a technique used in future studies called Causal Layered Analysis (CLA). It is designed to deepen understanding of the present and explore multiple possible futures. CLA divides issues into four distinct layers, which can be imagined as a step-by-step descent into the depths of the narrative map:[24]

1. **Litany:** This is the surface level of public discourse with everyday news and the issues that are most obvious.
2. **Social Causes:** This level delves deeper into exploring systemic perspectives and seeks to identify patterns over time.
3. **Worldview/Discourse:** This layer gets into the deep-seated cultural and cognitive reasons for the structures we observe.
4. **Myth/Metaphor:** The deepest layer is about the collective unconscious — the stories, myths, and metaphors that shape our worldviews.

Once the initial analysis is done, the process of CLA involves backcasting, where you start with a future scenario at the myth/metaphor level and then work backward to the present, figuring out the changes needed at each layer to achieve that future.

When translated into the narrative map, the CLA method begins on the left and incrementally explores deeper narratives based on cultural embeddedness. Once the present situation is adequately described, the future scenario is initially defined at the master narrative level, then gradually developed back toward emerging narratives. Here again, master narratives are viewed as powerful and invisible forces influencing our thinking, and any shift in thinking toward a different future must align with the existing master narrative landscape.

The CLA has been used over the years to analyze many different topics, including the Future of Water Resource Management in the Muslim World, a vision and strategy for Australia's minerals industry, an exploration of the Socio-Economic Aspirations of Singaporeans, and developing a narrative strategy for Germany's energy transformation.[25,26]

We've now completed the tour through narrative basics, narrative landscapes, and the mechanics of narrative change. In the next two chapters, I want to look at specific narratives for organizations, and we will start with the most important of all: the North Star narrative. For that, we look at one of the most inspiring industries and how it is redefining the capabilities of private companies.

SPACE

5. NORTH STAR NARRATIVES

THE PRIVATE RACE INTO SPACE

On Labor Day, 2001, Elon Musk was heading back to Manhattan from a weekend getaway in the Hamptons, accompanied by his college buddy Adeo Ressi. They were discussing Musk's aspirations following his exit from PayPal as a multi-millionaire. Musk had always harbored dreams of venturing into space, but it seemed like such a colossal and inaccessible feat — hardly something within the reach of a single individual. Yet, there was surely potential because, after all, a rocket is basically just metal and fuel, right?

That very evening, Musk went to the NASA website, expecting to find their plans for a Mars expedition. Given that humankind had set foot on the moon back in 1969, he presumed a Mars mission would be imminent. However, to his astonishment, not only was there no forthcoming schedule, but he also discovered that NASA had no immediate plans for Mars. The realization left him in disbelief and created the initial spark for his next endeavor.[1]

Walter Isaacson's biography of Elon Musk tells a great story about Musk's company SpaceX and how an impossible mission to create a private rocket company and go to space became a reality. Despite criticism for his frequent controversial comments on business, politics, and social issues, Musk exemplifies how to set big goals and solve hard technical problems with his companies. Musk started to learn about rocket engines and fuels and the challenges of space travel. At one point, he went to Russia and tried to buy two decommissioned Dnepr rockets. The deal did not happen, as the Russians kept increasing their price and even spat at Musk in an act of disrespect toward the young and inexperienced Silicon Valley millionaire. He went home with the conviction to build the rockets himself.

That idea seemed so far from what was possible for a private company that many of his friends repeatedly tried to talk him out of it. In the face of this doubt, his belief that humans could be a space-faring civilization amongst the stars was fueled. A vision was born: build a company that aspires to make humanity multi-planetary.[2]

THE FUTURE STARTS IN OUR DREAMS

Humans are most probably the only creatures capable of envisioning a distant future. While animals might anticipate events in the immediate future, it seems only Homo sapiens create narratives spanning years or centuries. Each of us has the ability to imagine our lives in five years, including our potential living situation, career, marriage, and family.

The further out we look, the less confident we feel. This is because, to a greater extent, it requires us to extrapolate from the present. We put a lot of effort into forecasting models of all kinds to make the future feel less unpredictable and cloudy, but all these efforts only go so far. The future is an opportunity space, a void that needs to be filled with our imagination.

There are many possible futures. Whoever has the ability to create a compelling narrative about the future will be in a prime position to actually shape it. Behind that insight is the concept of performativity: a particular vision of the future may turn out to become reality simply because a broad set of actors believe it to be probable. As a result, they orient their present behavior towards the imagined future as if it were already real. Expectations about the future can be seen as fundamentally generative — they are first created in our minds and then guide real activities and decisions.[3]

For instance, one future that is currently being played out is the role of remote work. The expectation that remote work will dominate the future of employment can shape corporate policies, technology development, and urban planning. Companies might invest in digital communication tools, develop policies for remote work, and reduce office space. As these changes take place, working remotely becomes more feasible and popular, leading to a shift in where people choose to live and how cities are designed. In this particular future, remote work would be the standard practice rather than an exception.

Peter Senge is a scientist at the MIT Sloan School of Management and is best known for his seminal book *The Fifth Discipline: The Art and Practice of the Learning Organization*. In the book, Senge emphasizes the importance of collective learning for businesses to be able to survive and outperform their peers. One of the disciplines he speaks of is to have a shared vision. Senge writes:

> A shared vision … may be inspired by an idea, but once it goes further — if it is compelling enough to acquire the support of more than one person — then it is no longer an abstraction. It is palpable. People begin to see it as if it exists. Few, if any, forces in human affairs are as powerful as a shared vision.[4]

Senge also notes that "vision" is a familiar concept in corporate leadership. But he argues that most "visions" are those of a single person (or group) imposed on an organization. Such visions, at best, command compliance — not commitment. A shared vision is one that many people are truly committed to because it reflects their own personal vision.

THE BEST VISION IS A NARRATIVE

What makes a vision powerful? How can organizations create visions that their members will truly commit to and make their own?

The ultimate destination for a vision is not your company website, a corporate slide deck, or a framed picture in the main lobby. It's the minds of the people that it brings together behind a common objective. A great vision is a narrative that people internalize and adopt as their personal narrative.

A strong organization always has a destination — something promising and unique that attracts employees, customers, and investors. A great North Star narrative can express what the organization aspires to achieve long-term, beyond just making money. Most importantly, the North Star narrative aligns and inspires employees to make the envisioned future happen. That's why it's the most important narrative for an organization.

Many organizations struggle with defining a compelling vision that creates commitment and alignment among their stakeholders. There are various concepts such as vision, mission, and purpose that continue to confuse strategy teams and, ultimately, employees and stakeholders. We will untangle these terms later in this chapter and unpack how the concept of a North Star narrative can integrate all of them into a much more understandable and coherent picture of the future.

A North Star narrative about the envisioned future of an organization is especially important in highly dynamic and changing environments. Emerging organizations like SpaceX, still in its early days, needed such a narrative to create a palpable fiction about the future because initially there wasn't much to show to investors, early employees, and customers.

A strong narrative about a future destination will also be vital for established organizations that need to change their way of doing things. Stories and the greater narratives they create are the way that we as humans conceive changes. When something changes, we can tell a story, draw people in, and make them care.

A GREAT NORTH STAR MAKES US CARE

Space travel has been a topic of debate for decades. Its supporters see it as a way to explore the unknown, expand our horizons, and advance our technology. Those who oppose space travel see it as a waste of time, money, and resources that could be better spent on solving the issues we face here on our own planet. This polarizing issue requires whoever does go to space to provide a clear and compelling reason as to why it's worthwhile.

SpaceX has merged its vision and mission into just one statement: Making Humanity Multiplanetary. It is an iconic vision — big and far out — but, at the same time, a very good definition of the end goal. There will hopefully be a moment many years from now when we all stare in awe at a screen in front of us as we witness the first human to ever set foot on another planet.[5]

You may argue that space and exploration companies have an advantage in creating great vision statements, as their industry is seemingly more exciting than developing software, managing nursing homes, or manufacturing appliances. While the thought of space exploration creates spectacular images in our minds, at the core, it's the power of the stories and the narratives behind space exploration and humanity that engages us and makes us care. Powerful strategic narratives between very similar companies can tell very different stories. Let's compare the strategic narrative of SpaceX with that of Blue Origin, a space technologies company launched just two years before SpaceX.

Blue Origin, an aerospace manufacturer and spaceflight company, was created by Amazon founder Jeff Bezos. Blue Origin's vision is clearly reflected in its name and its goal to move harmful industries into space in order to preserve Earth, humanity's blue origin. Its vision statement is "For the Benefit of Earth."[6]

Compare both visions: "Making Humanity Multiplanetary" vs. "For the Benefit of Earth." How do you feel about each one? What images do they bring to your mind?

The SpaceX vision is bold and visionary, whereas the Blue Origin vision seems vague and doesn't instantly trigger strong emotions or excitement. Why is that?

Blue Origin's vision statement doesn't really resemble a narrative. Remember, a narrative has a basic structure of a beginning, a middle, and an end. It takes us on a journey from our normal status quo, through a catalytic event, ultimately resulting in a new normal. Many vision statements that fail to capture our attention have blurry goals about an end state, like becoming the market leader. But the beginning of a story does something that is vitally important: it makes us care. In the words of professional storyteller and coach Kindra Hall:

> A bad story has a single, defining characteristic. We don't care. Even the flashiest of colors, the biggest of budgets, or the cutest of puppies can't make us care. They might get our attention, but they can't make us invest emotionally. They can't influence and transform. Fortunately, the majority of the time the root cause of this disconnect can be traced back to a single mistake, leaving out the first part of the story. The normal.[7]

A good story, in contrast, helps us connect by giving us a clear beginning, middle, and end. For instance, any memorable movie will introduce an identifiable character that captivates us and keeps us interested in their journey. As soon as this character gets into trouble, we start to care. We stick with the story until the end.

The SpaceX vision makes us care because we are all aware of the beginning of the story: Humans have never set foot on another planet. We landed on the moon a couple of times, but that was decades ago, and to really begin to conquer our solar system, we need to go to another planet. This is the beginning of the story. It is not specifically mentioned in the SpaceX vision, but that's not necessary because it's universal knowledge and part of the existing narrative landscape.

Compare that to the Blue Origin vision: what is the beginning of the story here? Is space travel being used for the first time for the benefit of Earth? There are already thousands of satellites orbiting Earth, benefitting our communications, weather data, navigation, and real-time observation. None of that is new. The Blue Origin vision isn't just vague in terms of the goal or the end of the story. It also misses the beginning, the challenge that makes us care.

A great vision connects the present with the future and therefore needs the structure of a starting state, a catalyst, and then an end state that we can relate to and picture in our mind. As previously discussed, this might not be completely spelled out, but it should be easily possible to construct a narrative from the vision.

Another major distinguishing factor of inspiring vs. uninspiring strategic narratives is their fit into the narrative landscape. Let's look at the narrative landscape of space travel and compare how SpaceX and Blue Origin resonate with their vision statements.

A GREAT NORTH STAR FITS INTO THE NARRATIVE LANDSCAPE

Blue Origin and SpaceX differ not just in their vision but also in their commercial approach and culture. These differences lead to a much better alignment of one of the two companies with the current and emerging narrative landscape and, as I argue, consequently to long-term competitive advantages.

Both teams aim to make space travel safer and more cost-effective by developing reusable rockets. This is a long and painstaking process. A space company needs many launches to both reduce fixed development and operations costs and to innovate and build better technology. Blue Origin has developed its New Shepard rocket as a reusable launch platform for space tourism. It can launch up to six people to the borderline between Earth's atmosphere and outer space, where they will experience weightlessness for about 10 minutes at a price tag of about $1.25 million USD per seat.[8]

SpaceX also offers space tourism, but their main driver for launches is Starlink, a satellite-based high-speed internet service for people living in remote and rural locations around the globe. It uses a constellation of thousands of satellites that orbit the planet much more closely than traditional satellites, which leads to lower latency and fast internet access. Starlink received global attention and well-deserved praise when it was deployed to Ukraine after Russia invaded the country in February 2022. Ukraine used it to stay connected to the internet and control their drones. However, SpaceX limited Ukraine's ability to use Starlink for military purposes, citing its policies.[9]

Both companies also compete for NASA and defense contracts, but SpaceX has a clear advantage as it already transports astronauts to the International Space Station. NASA also chose SpaceX to develop a lunar lander based on its Starship vehicle for the Artemis mission. Through Artemis, NASA intends to explore much more of the Moon and prepare for future astronaut missions to Mars. In May 2023, Blue Origin was awarded a contract to become the second provider for the Artemis mission. NASA's intention behind this apparent duplication of work is to foster a competitive approach that will ideally drive innovation and lower costs.[10]

Gradatim Ferociter is the Latin motto of Blue Origin. It means "step by step, ferociously." According to Bezos, "Basically, you can't skip steps, you have to put one foot in front of the other, things take time, there are no shortcuts, but you want to do those steps with passion and ferocity."[11]

Elon Musk started his career building software and he brought his best practices for faster and cheaper agile technological development to SpaceX. His team has been known to embrace failure, they work transparently, and grant access to bloggers and YouTubers to let a wider audience witness their progress as well as their failures. SpaceX's most watched video on the company's YouTube channel is entitled "How Not to Land an Orbital Rocket Booster." It is a compilation of the many failures their team experienced before they could finally celebrate a successful landing in December 2015.[12]

So far, the number of successful launches and the complexity of the missions completed speak for SpaceX. Despite being founded two years later the company has achieved a great technological advantage over Blue Origin. American theoretical physicist Michio Kaku argued that SpaceX has a "tremendous lead" over Blue Origin in regard to space exploration: "It's not head-to-head like the media would like to portray, you know, the battle of the billionaires. SpaceX has a tremendous lead over Blue Origin. They've been around the Earth several times, they go to the space station ... So none of this, going up for three minutes and coming back down. No, we're talking about the moon now."[13]

How do both approaches align with the narrative landscape for space travel and exploration? As stated before, the narrative map could consist of dozens of narratives. I will focus on a few select ones which specifically show the differences between both companies.

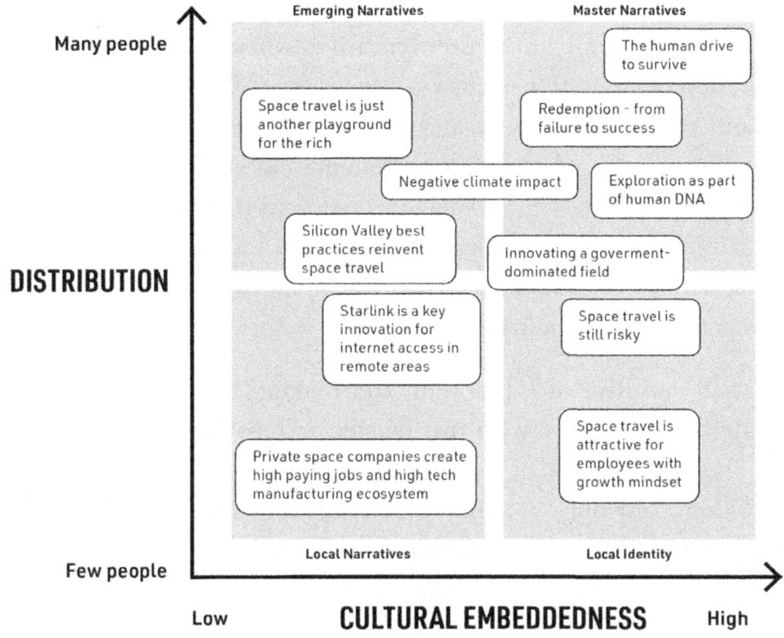

A narrative map for space travel

I will first explore the master narratives at play here, before moving on to emerging narratives (both emerging and local) and finally personal narratives.

There is a **master narrative** that favors both SpaceX and Blue Origin because they are private companies entering a sector that has until recently been dominated by government pursuits. The dominant space industry player in the United States, NASA, is a government agency with comparatively long development cycles and high launch costs. Americans have one of the most individualistic cultures in the world, which means they value independence and autonomy without much government or societal interference. Many Americans believe that the government is trying to do too many things that can be done more efficiently by private companies and individuals.

This goes hand in hand with the often iconic status of US entrepreneurs such as John D. Rockefeller or Steve Jobs, as they embody the spirit of innovation, risk-taking, and opportunism that has shaped the country's history and culture. Therefore, any entrepreneurial spirit that brings innovation to one of the last government-dominated areas can be expected to be met with a great deal of public support.[14]

One of the other dominant master narratives when it comes to space travel is exploration. Exploration is an essential part of human nature because it reflects our curiosity, creativity, and desire to understand ourselves and our place in the universe. According to genetic and sociological research, the human drive to "get out there" may well be driven by our DNA, as well as by necessity, evolution, and logic. Humans are uniquely suited to become explorers, with a set of traits such as great mobility, extraordinary dexterity, and brains that can think imaginatively.[15]

The SpaceX narrative of exploration and making humanity multiplanetary clearly aligns much more with this master narrative compared to the more limited "For the Benefit of Earth" vision of Blue Origin. In Elon Musk's words: "There are only a handful of really big milestones: single-celled life, multicellular life, differentiation of plants and animals, life extending from the oceans to land, mammals, consciousness. On that scale, the next important step is obvious: making life multiplanetary."[16]

SpaceX also benefits greatly from the structural master narrative of redemption, which involves overcoming failures and challenges to achieve success and glory. A Netflix documentary about the company tells the story of the first three launches of their Falcon 1 rocket, which failed, and a fourth and final attempt made with the last of their funding. Thankfully, that fourth launch was a success.

Blue Origin does not connect its stories to redemption. The company was much more secretive in general about its early development and progress. Blue Origin had a major incident in 2022 when an unmanned rocket crashed back to Earth shortly after liftoff, but the capsule carrying experiments managed to parachute to safety.[17] The unplanned but successful demonstration of the capsule rescue system can be seen as a great technological success and a big leap in safety for space travel. There are a lot of videos of the incident on the internet, however, none of them are shared or commented on by Blue Origin's own YouTube channel. Having space tourism as a business model, it might be reasonable to want to avoid pictures of exploding rockets and failures. Still, this positioning deprives Blue Origin of a powerful way to tell stories about the challenges they are overcoming.

What's left is the potentially most fundamental master narrative of them all — the drive for any kind of living creature to survive. Animals, humans, organizations, and societies have a deep desire to be around for another day, year, or century. Right now, we are alone in the universe, and whatever we achieve as humanity will be gone if our planet is destroyed or becomes uninhabitable. Being able to explore space could make a difference for ensuring the survival of our species. This is indeed a specific motivation for SpaceX as Musk agrees: "If we are able to go to other planets, the probable lifespan of human consciousness is going to be far greater than if we are stuck on one planet that could get hit by an asteroid or destroy its civilization."[18]

Overall, SpaceX achieves a significantly better fit to the master narrative landscape. Both companies have been founded by iconic entrepreneurs, and they showcase the fact that private initiative and innovation can challenge the traditional model of centralized, government-directed space activity. SpaceX forges ahead with its compelling vision and stories that connect to the powerful and deeply rooted master narratives of exploration, redemption, and survival as a species.

Now let's shift focus to **emerging narratives** that are linked with space travel. They can either be widespread such as emerging narratives or they can have a limited local scope. In order to simplify the analysis, we will focus on the more widely discussed issues. These are environmental impact, space tourism as the last frontier for multi-millionaires, and the actual good that these endeavors produce right now.

Space travel has a negative impact on the climate. Rockets need to burn a lot of propellant to lift off and reach space, which can release carbon dioxide and other pollutants such as soot and nitrous gasses into our atmosphere. Carbon dioxide is the main greenhouse gas contributing to global warming. Moreover, frequent rocket launches could also damage the ozone layer, which protects us from harmful ultraviolet radiation. However, both companies are trying to reduce their environmental footprint by developing rocket engines that use carbon-neutral fuels. This means they are trying to minimize or even neutralize the negative impact of this important narrative on their business.[19]

Blue Origin even attempts to use this narrative in a positive way with its vision statement and its intention to move harmful industries from the surface of the Earth to space. However, this narrative currently lacks concrete examples of how Blue Origin's activities actually benefit the planet or its inhabitants, as most of the focus and stories so far have been on space tourism. This is a good example of a potentially powerful narrative that remains "hollow" for now because it lacks concrete stories and evidence to actually build credibility for the vision.

Silicon Valley is a world-renowned hub for technology and entrepreneurship that has developed a unique culture of innovation, fostering creativity, collaboration, and risk-taking. One of the key aspects of this culture is agility. Methodologies and books such as *The Lean Startup* by Eric Ries have created a global movement with new types of agile companies that are faster and more innovative than their competitors because they embrace uncertainty, experiment with new ideas, and learn from their failures.

SpaceX brings this philosophy to a risk-averse, slow, and expensive industry and builds a technological advantage that is years ahead of the market. This story and narrative resemble that of another of Musk's companies, one that is deeply disrupting the automotive industry: Tesla. SpaceX even brought the Silicon Valley geek culture to space operations by sending a Tesla car with a puppet astronaut as test payload into orbit as well as naming their Atlantic and Pacific Ocean landing drone ships "Just Read the Instructions (JRTI)" and "Of Course I Still Love You (OCISLY)."

The resulting positive narrative is that "SpaceX brings Silicon Valley best practices to another old industry." This is good news for all SpaceX stakeholders, such as customers who expect lower costs, investors who see the disruptive potential, and employees who want to work in a place where they can quickly learn and grow. This narrative connects to the master narrative of redemption and enhances it with modern philosophy. There will be challenges because things move fast and experiments are embraced.

Blue Origin is not using this agile messaging because they focus on safety as their top mission and use "step by step, ferociously" as their approach. Flying humans to space is a great responsibility, even more so if they are tourists and not professional astronauts. Choosing space tourism as their initial launch focus not only necessitated that safety be a front-and-center message, but also created another narrative challenge to address: the growing inequality in our societies.

Scientific American's Senior Editor Clara Moskovitz wrote an article in 2022 entitled "Billionaire Space Tourism Has Become Insufferable" which argued that space travel has shifted "from brave exploration to just another playground for the 0.0000001 percent." This issue hit a nerve especially because shortly before, in July 2021, another billionaire, Richard Branson, had also traveled to space with his company Virgin Galactic, doing so at the same time many ordinary people were exhausted with strained finances in the middle of the COVID-19 pandemic.[20]

Blue Origin is trying to counter this challenge by telling stories about space tourists and their achievements and dreams. These stories might be personal and emotional, but it's hard to forget the negative narrative of the excesses of the rich because the journey to space is such an incredible privilege for a tiny fraction of humanity.

SpaceX is in a much better place in the narrative landscape here. This is because its main activity does not center around tourism, but rather global internet access with the Starlink offering. Moreover, the indispensable role of the Starlink network for the defense of Ukraine has even credibly connected the activities of SpaceX to Blue Origin's vision, "For the Benefit of Earth." It is not the main vision of SpaceX, but for now, they have filled it with more life and actual stories compared to Blue Origin.

Summarizing the emerging narratives category, we see SpaceX prevail here as well, with two connections to positive emerging narratives compared to Blue Origin's one rather negative connection to supporting the excesses of the rich.

Finally, there are **personal narratives**, which we define as evolving stories that are created in our minds. Personal narratives are harder to analyze as they happen in our brains, but thankfully, there is data available from Glassdoor, a platform where employees can give public feedback to the companies where they work. This is from a review left by a SpaceX technician in early 2023 on Glassdoor:

> **Pros**
>
> Hard-working team moving towards a common goal. Have shared some happy tears with coworkers watching our company make history.
>
> **Cons**
>
> Long hours will test you to no end. The culture in SpaceX will either help you to thrive or eat you alive — no in betweens. Lots of drop off due to this.
>
> **Advice to Management**
>
> Nothing, we are all doing the best we can! Ad astra!

As of December 2023, Glassdoor shows more than 3,000 reviews for SpaceX and 724 for Blue Origin. Individual reviews are always very subjective opinions of single employees, which are influenced by their teams, line managers, and work environment. However, there is a rating scale of one to five stars for important aspects of the employee experience that can be aggregated and provides a data-driven perspective on personal narratives.

The overall rating is 3.8 for SpaceX and 3.5 for Blue Origin, with higher rates representing a more favorable review. A few categories like Culture & Values, Diversity & Inclusion, Compensation and Benefits, and Career Opportunities are very similar for both. Things are different for Senior Management with a rating of 3.3 for SpaceX vs. 2.6 for Blue Origin, and Work/Life Balance with a whopping difference of 2.6 for SpaceX vs 3.7 for Blue Origin.

In addition, Glassdoor asks reviewers to give approval ratings on a percentage basis for the CEO and the future positive business outlook. Here, SpaceX leads the CEO approval rating with 82 percent vs. 35 percent approval for Blue Origin CEO Bob Smith, as well as the positive business outlook rating at 80 percent compared to Blue Origin's 52 percent.

Based on these numbers, SpaceX seems to be a workplace where employees are fairly confident that their leadership team will steer the company toward a positive future with the notable downside of less work/life balance. Blue Origin creates a comparably better work/life balance, which is also reflected in many of the individual reviews. However, the leadership ratings and future outlook are significantly lower compared to SpaceX.

As an employer brand, SpaceX achieves vertical integration between master narratives, emerging narratives, and individual narratives for a specific audience: people who seek growth opportunities and who are willing to go the extra mile. The combined SpaceX narrative could be summarized like this:

> There are few visions greater than making humanity multiplanetary. We do this with a culture that was born in Silicon Valley and has helped countless companies to become undisputed market leaders in their field. Working at SpaceX means growing every day and going the extra mile, but it is incredibly rewarding as you will work with world-class talent to change the future of humanity.

Considering Blue Origin's narrative in the same light, it struggles to match the captivating levels of storytelling from SpaceX. Blue Origin struggles to connect positively to the existing narrative landscape with its vision. It is still a very attractive employer, especially considering the employees' much better work/life balance, but SpaceX might be the more attractive employer overall, especially for talent with a strong growth mindset. Over the long term, this can have an influence on further extending the competitive advantage that SpaceX has today.

Blue Origin's opportunity lies in securing contracts such as those awarded by NASA. This might provide new opportunities to better connect the vision to the narrative landscape and tell stories beyond space tourism. For example, an adapted vision from "For the Benefit of Earth" to "Exploring Space to Protect Earth" would already introduce a connection to the exploration master narrative and make clear that supporting our planet with insights and resources from space is not a nice-to-have but an essential part of the plan to allow humanity to survive and thrive on our blue origin.

HOW TO DEFINE VISION AND MISSION WITH THE NORTH STAR NARRATIVE

It seems like every organization has a different method when it comes to declaring its reason for being. Some just have a mission statement. Some have a vision statement and a mission statement. Some just have a declared purpose, and many are using all three together. If you google mission, vision, and purpose, you will get an endless list of explanations trying to differentiate the terms and concepts from each other. Here's a brief summary:

A **vision statement** is typically used to paint an aspirational picture of the future. For example, the vision of the Alzheimer's Association is "A world without Alzheimer's and all other dementia."[21]

A **mission statement** explains how an organization plans to achieve this vision. It answers the "how" — the actions, behaviors, and strategies that will bring the vision to life. The mission of the Alzheimer's Association is to "lead the way to end Alzheimer's and all other dementia — by accelerating global research, driving risk reduction and early detection, and maximizing quality care and support."

A **purpose statement** is a more recent trend that specifically tries to provide an answer to the question: "Why does our organization exist?" As I will argue later, I believe that a good vision and mission statement can make a purpose statement obsolete.

No matter what combination of mission, vision, and purpose an organization implements, a strategy on paper is only the starting point for engaging all those who will implement it. Strategies must also be communicated and understood, and they must motivate action. The most important feature of a strategic direction is that it actually reaches the minds of the people who are supposed to bring it to life. It's of no use as a genius idea in the minds of a few top leaders. MIT Sloan School of Management research found that only 28 percent of managers could correctly name their firm's strategic priorities.[22] If managers don't understand the strategic direction, imagine how bleak these numbers get for employees in the office or even on the frontline. A clear strategic direction helps the entire workforce understand why they do what they do. It inspires and motivates them.

The concept of a North Star narrative creates even more clarity and impact on the way organizations communicate their vision, mission, and purpose. Here are six insights on how to make this happen:

1. **A great vision should follow a narrative form and make us care.**

   As we have seen before, the more a vision follows a narrative form, the more we care. We care because there is a normal, old way of doing things, and then something happens that ultimately leads to a new normal. The Alzheimer's Association's vision "A world without Alzheimer's and all other dementia" does not necessarily need to state the normal here because most of us know that Alzheimer's is a serious disease without a cure. Many people have heard stories of how dementia only worsens over time and how dramatically it impacts the quality of life for patients and their families. This is why a world without Alzheimer's and all other dementia is such a big, important, and aspirational goal for all humans.

   The Staffbase vision is, "In a polarized world, we inspire people to achieve great things together." Talking about polarization is incredibly important for our vision because it points to a major challenge that we, as a society, are facing right now. Without it, the vision would lack impact and feel arbitrary.

2. **A great vision should be an inclusive narrative.**

   The former vision of a Fortune 500 company was as follows:

   > *We aspire to be the most admired and valuable company in the world.*

   This is not a good vision statement. It is too broad and general. But more importantly, it is self-centered. Shareholders might care about this vision, but what about employees, customers, or the communities in which this organization operates? They are not included. A good vision should talk about a future that's at the very least aspirational for all stakeholders and preferably invites people to join the movement: employees, customers, communities, and shareholders.

What's even more powerful is an inclusive vision of a future we all want to live in. By telling stakeholders a visionary narrative, organizations inspire those who share the same goals and beliefs. This naturally involves describing a shift that most likely cannot be pulled off by just one organization. The Alzheimer's Association is unlikely to achieve its very aspirational vision alone. That's what the mission of "accelerating global research, driving risk reduction and early detection, and maximizing quality care and support" is for. They know they cannot do this alone, but they want to be the leader and accelerate the process as much as possible.

The same applies to our Staffbase mission. It is "To help organizations unlock the power of inspirational communication so they can thrive in the Narrative Age." This is our concrete contribution to the far greater vision of inspiring people to achieve great things together in a polarized world.

3. A mission that's not connected to a vision lacks impact.

Quite a few organizations are just talking about their goals in terms of a mission. Translated to a narrative form, this would mean telling a story without the beginning and end. They just talk about the action or transformation that's happening without providing the context to explain why this transformation is essential.

As mentioned before, it is possible to leave out the vision if the existing narrative landscape helps the audience to understand the unspoken part of the story. The SpaceX mission to travel to other planets is very grand and relies on the implicit knowledge that humans have never before traveled to other planets. When John F. Kennedy promised in 1962 to put a man on the moon by the end of the century, everybody knew that no one had ever set foot on the moon.

In contrast, some missions need more explanation to make them impactful. Take, for example, the updated Starbucks mission, which was introduced in 2023:

With every *cup*,

With every *conversation*,

With every *community*—

We nurture the limitless possibilities of human connection.

What are the normal and new normal here? Isn't human connection something that we have all the time? Starbucks does not have a vision statement to help clarify this, and the existing narrative landscape does not help either. What's needed is a visionary context that supports the mission. CEO Laxman Narasimhan explains the "normal" in a post about the new mission on the Starbucks website:

> Study after study indicates high rates of loneliness as a public health concern, and there's a desperate need for togetherness. We live in a world that is highly disconnected, and loneliness, division, and polarization have become far too common ... The everyday ritual of coffee is a powerful way to connect — with yourself and with others."[23]

Once we understand the problem better, we start to care and understand what the Starbucks mission is all about. This is impactful because the narrative about loneliness as a growing and concerning health issue impacts all of us. Starbucks will not solve it alone, but connecting its mission to this broad and important vision is powerful.

Sometimes, a once-dominant narrative will fade into the background of the narrative landscape and create the need to redefine the vision. A common example is the European Union. Once, Europe had a story about moving past frequent internal wars by coming together and uniting more closely. But for Europeans born today into the "end of history" narrative without any personal link to those wars, this story unfortunately might not mean much. That's why European leaders right now need to build a new vision and North Star narrative about what Europe will be for the generations to come.[24]

4. Great visions do not need a purpose.

A vision should resonate with the narrative landscape of your stakeholders. It should connect to what they care about. In that case, there is no additional purpose statement needed. The Alzheimer's Association does not have a separate purpose statement because everyone immediately gets the purpose based on the vision and mission. In contrast, if a vision or mission doesn't address the why of an organization and an additional purpose statement is needed, that might be a sign of a limited, self-centered, or otherwise insufficient vision.

5. A North Star narrative can integrate vision and mission into one simple statement.

A major challenge of the vision and mission concept is that it forces the audience to first understand the difference between both concepts. That is confusing and distracts from the actual understanding of the strategic direction. Imagine sitting with a friend in a bar and getting asked what the company you just joined is all about and why you felt compelled to join. Nobody wants to hear an empty recitation of a mission and vision statement.

Andy Raskin, mentioned before as a consultant for strategic narratives, proposes a simple concept to talk about the strategic direction.[25] The idea is to integrate the vision and mission statement into a few short sentences that are easy to remember and simple to pass on. This approach was developed for business-to-business (B2B) models, but can also be applied to business-to-consumer (B2C) brands.

Andy defines three steps to create a strategic narrative:

1. Identify an undeniable change in the world, a move from an old way of doing things to a new way of thinking. The change might be caused by new opportunities such as technology or by new challenges such as an aging population.

2. Name the stakes. Paint a picture of why playing the old game is a road to ruin and joining the new game is a way to win. This is only needed if the change and its urgency and impact are not well known to your audience.
3. Share the goal state or the promised land you want your customers to help achieve.

A good vision statement fits well into the first part — what's the big change in the world that an organization is addressing? The mission statement fits the third part because it's about what you are actually doing to help usher in this change. The importance of the second part depends on the existing narrative landscape. If the vision is to end Alzheimer's disease, many may not need strong reminders of the stakes as they know this is a big deal. But some might not know, and therefore, the stakes need to be made more transparent. In the case of the Alzheimer's Association, this approach could be used to transform the vision and mission into a single statement.

> **Vision**: A world without Alzheimer's and all other dementia®
>
> **Mission**: The Alzheimer's Association leads the way to end Alzheimer's and all other dementia — by accelerating global research, driving risk reduction and early detection, and maximizing quality care and support.

Turned into a single strategic narrative for the Alzheimer's Association:

> We believe in a future without Alzheimer's and all other dementia. There are over 10 million new cases of dementia each year worldwide. One new case every 3.2 seconds. Our mission is to lead the way to end Alzheimer's and all other dementia — by accelerating global research, driving risk reduction and early detection, and maximizing quality care and support.

The numbers to show the annual global impact of dementia could be left out.[26] I added them to demonstrate how a strategic narrative could include details to better describe the problem that is solved and to quantify the difference between the current norm and the new normal in our narrative.

This is how the Starbucks mission statement could be turned into a narrative that includes the old way of doing things and the aspiration for the new way:

> We live in a world where loneliness, division, and polarization have become far too common. Humans need more and better ways to connect — with ourselves and with others. With every cup, with every conversation, with every community — we nurture the limitless possibilities of human connection.

These narratives might be longer than the original mission statement, but their narrative form makes it more meaningful and, therefore, easier to remember and pass on to others. The more the narrative is known and integrated into the narrative landscape, the easier it is to start using simple slogans or symbols instead of the full narrative.

6. Narrative constellations support the North Star.

A narrative never stands entirely alone. It will connect and resonate within an existing narrative landscape. Moreover, narratives can be specifically organized into constellations to support and amplify each other. The metaphor of the narrative constellations is derived from astronomical constellations by narrative researchers such as Robert Schiller. No matter which cultures have looked at the starry sky, all saw patterns such as Ursa Minor, The Little Bear. These constellations are chance alignments of stars, but humans interpret them in a way that seems natural to the human mind.[27]

Narratives, like stars, can be arranged into constellations and benefit from complementary effects. The brightest star in your constellation is the North Star. It holds the constellation together and points the way to the future.

The main benefit of these constellations is that the narratives provide each other with credibility. Take, for example, SpaceX, with its long-term strategic narrative of landing on another planet. This vision seems very far away right now. However, there is another narrative in the constellation that is more focused on the near term and was able to show great progress in past years: building reusable rockets as a first step toward dramatically reducing the cost of going to space at scale. Every success with the reusable rockets, in turn, provides credibility for the larger narrative.

History can be another star in the constellation. Many companies use their history as an important narrative to talk about their identity and values. The first story Starbucks tells on its website is about the company's heritage, from opening its first store in 1971 on Seattle's historic Pike Place Market to reinventing its coffeehouse culture in the 1980s after being inspired by Italy's warm, artisanal coffeehouses. The heritage of a brand will most likely not be used as the strategic narrative, but it will remain an important part of many companies' narrative constellations.

While North Star narratives are a powerful way to inspire your stakeholders about the future, a company without a narrative moat may not survive long enough to fulfill its mission at all. In the next chapter, we take a deeper look at the different types of narratives that can create a narrative moat for a business. These narratives, too, become a part of the constellation and ideally connect back to the North Star, providing each other with credibility.

6. THE NARRATIVE MOAT

NOTHING LESS THAN A DIAMOND

When you envision a marriage proposal, what comes to mind? For many, it's the classic image of a gleaming diamond engagement ring. However, behind this symbol of love and commitment is a little-known secret: a diamond engagement ring dramatically loses its monetary value the moment it's purchased. As soon as that sparkling ring leaves the jewelry store, its financial worth plummets by at least 50 percent. But why, despite knowing this, do we remain so enchanted by diamonds? And how did they become synonymous with love and marriage?

Diamonds became popular in America about 75 years ago. It's an incredible story of market creation bolstered by a powerful narrative moat. At the heart of this tale is a single company founded in 1888: De Beers.

Diamonds weren't always considered rare. The 1870 discovery of vast diamond mines in South Africa threatened to saturate the market. Recognizing the potential crisis, British financiers behind the mining operations formed De Beers Consolidated Mines, Ltd. in 1888 with two objectives: monopolizing diamond prices and stabilizing the market. Under the leadership of Sir Ernest Oppenheimer, De Beers took control of the diamond trade, strategically stockpiling and selling diamonds to maintain desired prices.[1]

However, controlling supply was only half the battle. To truly dominate, they needed to manage demand, and for this, De Beers identified the US as the ideal market for growth, despite diamond sales having plummeted there after World War I.

De Beers conducted deep market research, discovering that in the late 1930s, diamonds were viewed as luxuries for the elite. They had to alter this perception to increase diamond sales, making diamonds desirable to people across various income levels. Their solution? Link diamonds to emotions, specifically love and commitment. They aimed to make diamonds synonymous with engagement, ensuring they were not just seen as precious stones but as irreplaceable tokens of love.[2]

At the campaign's core was the timeless slogan, "A diamond is forever." This slogan, according to AdAge, was the #1 slogan of the 20th century, encapsulating everything De Beers wanted to convey: the eternity of love and the lasting value of diamonds. It also subtly dissuaded people from reselling their diamonds.

Before this campaign, only 10 percent of engagement rings held diamonds. Over the years, De Beers not only transformed this number dramatically but even influenced how much one should spend on an engagement ring. The "two months' salary" rule, suggesting one should spend two months' wages on a ring, was another of their successful marketing ploys.[3]

Today, the diamond industry is valued at nearly $100 billion USD annually, with more than 50 percent of polished diamonds globally sold in the US.[4,5] De Beers didn't just market a product; they marketed values, emotions, and societal norms by creating a powerful narrative about the eternal emotional value of a diamond. There is of course plenty about which to be critical regarding the ways De Beers manipulated scarcity while simultaneously exploiting African labor and resources in their rise to market dominance.

In the late 1990s, however, the company took steps to amend for some of its past offenses. These measures were welcomed by human rights groups and have been subsequently adopted by many other companies in the diamond industry.[6]

Do you remember the three types of master narratives discussed in Chapter 3: biographical, structural, and episodic? Buying an engagement ring that is expensive enough to require some financial effort, potentially even months of saving, has become a biographical master narrative in the United States. It is a visual representation of the love and commitment one has in their relationship. When somebody gets engaged, the engagement ring plays an important cultural role in the process. That's a biographical master narrative at work. Master narratives are deeply rooted and hard to create. It took De Beers a decades-long campaign and dedication to the same messaging and narrative over time: diamonds are the ultimate physical sign of love and commitment, and they are forever.

Because De Beers had monopolized the diamond market, there was no need to advertise a specific diamond brand. They just had to create demand for diamonds and ensure people kept them as long as possible because reselling would put pressure on prices. As a result, these deep-rooted narratives created a competitive moat around a whole industry.

THE NARRATIVE MOAT

As defined in Chapter 1, a "moat" in a business context is a company's competitive advantage that is difficult for competitors to imitate or overcome. It protects the business much like a moat protects a castle. Strong narratives are able to build long-lasting competitive advantages for organizations. The core of the moat is the North Star narrative, which points to the future and creates a destination for the organization to reach.

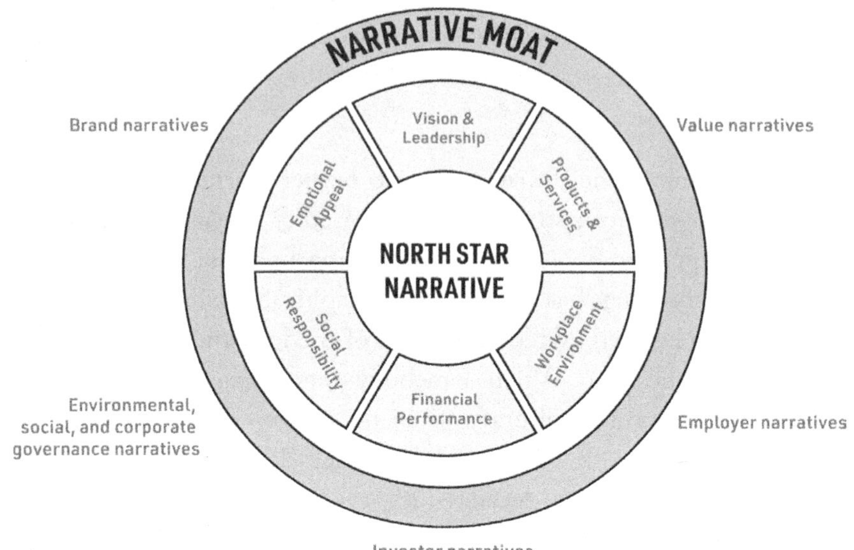

The North Star is relevant for all stakeholders, but it is first and foremost targeted at employees because reputation is built from the inside out. Customers, potential employees, investors, and the public may need more specific narratives that build the organization's reputation as an exciting brand, a great employer, a long-term investment, and a responsible part of society.

Let's take a closer look at which key narratives and audiences play an important role in building the narrative moat.

INCREASING THE PERCEIVED VALUE FOR CUSTOMERS

A leather bag from Louis Vuitton costs between $2,000 and $40,000 USD. The estimated production cost of one bag is between $200 USD on the lower end and up to $800 USD for very special cases.[7] Louis Vuitton marks up the price between 800 and 2,000 percent, which means customers pay thousands of dollars for nothing more than — a narrative!

The world of luxury brands provides stunning examples of how customer-focused narratives are increasing the perceived value of products or services.

The common term is "value story," even though the story is usually in fact a narrative because it is built up over time by many stories or factual pieces of information coalescing.

Luxury brands often curate a rich tapestry of stories that trace back to their origins, emphasizing their enduring legacy, the craftsmen's unparalleled skills, and the brand's journey through time. This narrative is artfully communicated through marketing campaigns, store experiences, and product design.

Louis Vuitton began its journey in 1854 in Paris, founded by its namesake, as a small workshop specializing in crafting custom luxury trunks. With his innovative flat-topped trunks, a stark contrast to the domed bags of the era, Vuitton revolutionized the world of luggage and became an iconic global brand.

For Louis Vuitton customers, each purchase isn't just a transaction; it's an induction into a storied legacy. One of the key strengths of a narrative comes into play here. A story is mainly about other people, but a narrative is inclusive; it is possible to join the movement. I can buy a Louis Vuitton leather bag or a Tiffany's necklace and acquire a piece of history and a status symbol. Purchasing a luxury good is an investment into an aspirational vision of ourselves.

Value narratives are not limited to the world of luxury and decades of brand campaigns and heritage building. They can also elevate an otherwise subpar customer experience in a much shorter time frame. One of the most outstanding examples in the past few years comes from Berlin Public Transport, which managed nothing less than turning customer hate into love.

In 2015, Berlin Public Transport (BVG) faced a challenge. Despite numerous marketing campaigns, the sentiment around using BVG was negative. Nearly 47 percent of its customers admitted they hated using the service! Martell Beck was the BVG Head of Sales and Marketing at BVG and he knew that changing the company's service wasn't an easy or immediate option. Buses got stuck in traffic like any other vehicle, and ordering a new subway car could take seven years from order to delivery. The issue was further complicated by the city's increasing traffic brought on by its rapid growth. Instead of focusing solely on service modifications, BVG needed to invest in changing public perception.[8]

The result was a campaign named "Because we love you" which aimed to make it fashionable to use BVG transportation in Berlin. To engage with a younger audience and open a dialogue with its customers, BVG turned to social media to launch the campaign. On January 13, 2015, they invited users to share their best BVG moments. The response was a massive backlash. What started as a handful of tweets became a trending topic, with headlines like "The idiots at BVG beg for love." At the end of the first day, this shitstorm even reached national media outlets, and everyone was criticizing BVG's approach.

But instead of retreating, BVG saw an opportunity. This was their first campaign that genuinely reached and moved people. It was just day one, and the actual campaign hadn't even started yet. BVG doubled down on their efforts. Instead of backtracking, they decided to continue with their campaign and focused on aligning their messages with the existing narrative landscape of customers and Berliners.

It became evident that addressing and changing the personal narratives of its customers in the short term was nearly impossible. The sight of delayed services, unkempt trains, and impolite drivers was too entrenched in people's minds.

However, as a city, Berlin held a unique master narrative of being "cool but a bit dysfunctional." Berliners have embraced this characterization for years, echoing the earlier narrative of being "poor but sexy."

A big and bustling city like Berlin also creates a particular type of personal identity for its inhabitants. Research suggests that Berliners are more inclined to race after buses and trains than those in Munich, even though the frequency of public transportation in Berlin is more regular. Sociologist Martina Löw introduced the theory that cities have a unique "logic" that influences and shapes their residents. Put simply, life in big cities often makes inhabitants more impatient, a behavioral trait confirmed by her neuroscientific studies. Consequently, public transportation customers in big cities will likely always complain about the frequency of the service and never be happy with what they have.[9]

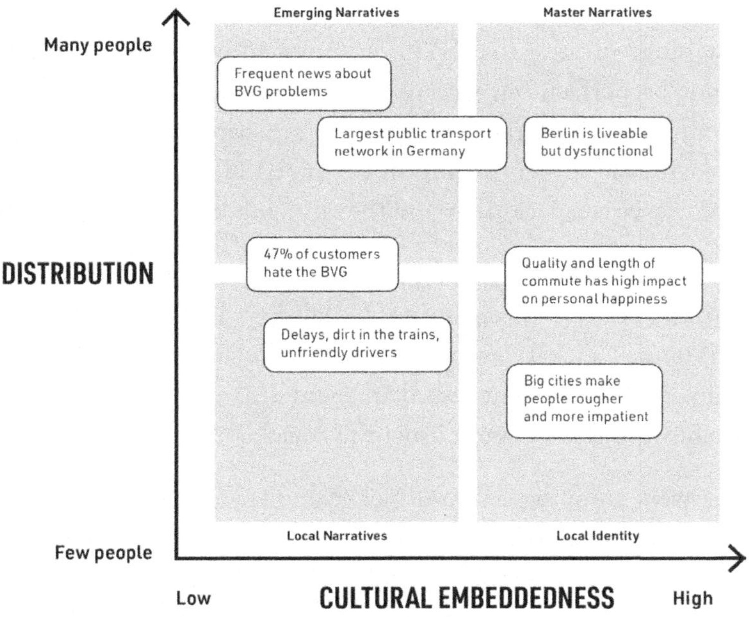

The narrative map for Berlin Public Transport (BVG) in 2015

Recognizing these narratives, BVG began crafting messages that were self-critical, reflecting their challenges while also highlighting their commitment. For instance, when Ringo Starr held a concert in Berlin, BVG's advertisement humorously remarked:

> *Ringo Starr is in town. Finally, someone who's worse at keeping the beat than we are.*

Another example addressed the frustration impatient BVG customers had with ticket machines:

> *In Terminator 6, humans fight against machines. You can experience that every day at our ticket machines.*

This type of messaging, which was echoed throughout their campaigns, resonated with Berliners. BVG acknowledged its shortcomings but also humorously held up a mirror to its customers.

The overarching narrative that BVG championed was: "We are like Berlin. We may not be perfect, but we are genuine, lovable, and steadfast in our commitment. Every day, rain or shine, we are here for you." By aligning themselves with the authentic spirit of Berlin, BVG successfully bridged the gap between service expectations and the city's inherent narrative landscape.

BVG also introduced everyday topics onto the public agenda and took a clear position. For instance, during Equal Pay Day, they introduced a cheaper "Women's Ticket," emphasizing the gender pay gap where women in Germany earn 21 percent less than men. This campaign drew massive attention, showing BVG's commitment to social issues.

The results were stunning. From a Net Promoter Score of -10, BVG rose to +18. This change wasn't just in numbers but also in public perception across all age groups. Ticket sales surged, with BVG's growth rate doubling that of the city. This success was attributed not just to the service but also to the campaign. And it didn't just impact customers. For the BVG staff, the campaign had a significant impact too. Employees were proud to be associated with the company, feeling that the marketing wasn't just for customers but also for them. The campaign strengthened the employer brand and significantly increased job applications.

BVG's journey from a negatively perceived public service to a beloved brand in Berlin underscores the power of understanding audience sentiment, the potential of social media, and the importance of genuine customer engagement. Understanding the narrative landscape and building a value narrative and messaging that resonated perfectly inspired customers and transformed BVG's image.

BUILDING A DISTINCTIVE EMPLOYER BRAND

> *Recruiting, by its very nature, is the most important thing HR organizations do. If you aren't finding the best, brightest, and most aligned people to join your company, all the other management and business process work will fail.*[10] — Josh Bersin

In the war for talent, many companies are focusing solely on pay, perks, and benefits, but that's not enough to stand out. Narratives can have a huge impact on how attractive and distinctive an organization appears to be to potential employees. They are critical to defining the employer brand and clearly articulating the employer value proposition (EVP) that sets an organization apart.

SpaceX is a prime example of two key ways that narratives can benefit employer brands. First, a compelling North Star narrative is a strong driver for being a desirable employer, which allows employees to link their work to a larger positive and exciting impact. As SpaceX engineer Blaine Allen writes on X, formerly known as Twitter:[11]

> Someone asked me, "How can you want to work for SpaceX, Elon is so controversial?"
>
> I replied that the mission of SpaceX is a hell of a lot bigger than a single person. He's one man of ~12,000 hard working builders ... Even if my part is small, that's a mission I want to wake up early to help make a reality for my future children.

Second, traditional employer branding is deeply rooted in the world of marketing and consumer branding. The objective is to increase the size of the audience as much as possible and to create a sale from every prospect. Talent acquisition however has completely inverted goals. It's not about giving a job to everyone. Bryan Adams and Charlotte Marshall are employer branding experts and have written a book about this philosophy entitled *Give & Get Employer Branding: Repel the Many and Compel the Few with Impact, Purpose and Belonging.*

They argue that "The best employer brands are the ones that are who they are in a public (and human) way. If you don't like what you see, sorry. If you do, you will love working here."[12] According to this view, employer branding is closer to online dating than to online selling — finding the right fit instead of attracting masses of people. Recruiting fails when everyone is attracted. For instance, the global investment bank Goldman Sachs is known for its demanding work culture, often involving long hours. This narrative draws criticism for the missing work-life balance, especially for analysts in their first years at the bank. However, it also attracts highly ambitious individuals who view the intensity as a challenge and an opportunity to learn and prove themselves in a competitive environment.

This approach requires a narrative change from "It's easy to work here with all the benefits and opportunities" to "Do you have what it takes to work here?" The employer branding narrative should repel those who won't fit in and attract better-matched people to apply. Adams and Marshall believe that telling an authentic story about what happens behind the curtain will not just attract the right candidates but a lot more of them:

> For an organization that appreciates the value of happy, productive people to achieve business success, this approach is extremely valuable. The beauty of this is, 49 percent of candidates consciously cite knowing what it's really like to work somewhere as the number one obstacle to changing jobs. And 66 percent of candidates want to know about the culture and values most of all.[13]

CONVINCING SHAREHOLDERS TO INVEST

In the complex investing world, numbers and analytics play a pivotal role. However, the influence of the narrative behind a stock can be just as potent in shaping investor perceptions and decisions. The term "story stock" has emerged to define those companies whose share value is driven more by the compelling narrative surrounding their potential than by traditional financial fundamentals like assets and income. Such stocks often have valuations that surpass what their current financial metrics might justify, primarily due to investors' optimistic expectations regarding the company's future. These stocks are often found in dynamic sectors like technology or biotechnology and often receive abundant media coverage.

One of the most well-known story stocks in recent years is GameStop, a retailer specializing in video games. The company's stock became incredibly popular among retail investors, particularly those organizing on social media platforms like Reddit. A large number of these small investors collectively bought shares and options, driving the share price from under $20 USD at the beginning of 2021 to around $480 USD at its peak. The company's market capitalization rose to over $20 billion USD. Since several hedge funds had bet on the stock's decline through short sales, they incurred billions in losses during the price increase. This phenomenon even became a Netflix documentary titled *Eat the Rich: The GameStop Saga.*

But not all story stocks are a fad. The rise and sustained performance of tech giants, often termed FAANG (Facebook, Amazon, Apple, Netflix, Google), is a testament to the potential of story stocks. These companies, once story stocks themselves, have demonstrated impressive performance since their inception. For instance, when Facebook went public in 2012, there was a tremendous amount of interest in its potential to dominate social media, expand its user base globally, and innovate in digital advertising. The company's valuation was significantly driven by its growth story and less so by existing revenue generation. Over time, Facebook demonstrated its ability to monetize its platform through advertising.

While the term "story stock" refers explicitly to stocks with a future-oriented outlook and high anticipated growth rates, the power of a compelling narrative is vital for every company. Possessing a clear story and vision about delivering value to a growing addressable market in the future can significantly influence how financial markets and investors perceive a company. The more effectively leaders can convey this narrative, the more it enhances the company's valuation and support from investors.

The influence of narratives isn't limited to publicly traded companies. For startups struggling to get off the ground, the story is often all they have. Without a track record or substantial financial data, these young companies rely heavily on their narrative to attract venture capital. Investors bet on the narrative's potential to materialize into a profitable reality. While some startups successfully transform their narrative into tangible success, many need to catch up, underscoring the speculative nature of such investments.

It's worth noting once again that the power of narratives can be used to mislead investors and excite them about a business venture without carefully looking into the details. Startups like Theranos, which lied about a supposedly breakthrough technology for blood tests, or the cryptocurrency exchange FTX, which failed in its risk management, are recent examples of charismatic founders who manipulated and misled investors with irresistible visions of a bright future.

OBTAINING THE LICENSE TO OPERATE

The growing awareness of the finite nature of our world's resources, the impact of climate change, and the detrimental effects of many human actions on our environment have made this domain a top priority for every organization. Consequently, this area also becomes a temptation to deceive and manipulate through simplistic narratives.

The term "greenwashing" describes the practice in which companies present themselves as more environmentally friendly or ethical than they truly are. Oil companies launch advertising campaigns focusing on their investment in renewable energy, while the bulk of their investment and operations remain heavily in fossil fuel extraction. Clothing brands release "sustainable" clothing lines, using a small percentage of recycled materials, yet continue to engage in practices that contribute to water pollution or poor labor conditions in the majority of their operations.

When it comes to greenwashing, straws are a common example. In 2019, McDonald's introduced paper straws in the UK that turned out to be non-recyclable. In the UK, 4.7 billion straws are used annually, but they make up just 0.025 percent of total plastic waste in the ocean. Straws are an easy target at which companies can aim a sustainable narrative; they're a wasteful plastic product that consumers are highly aware of.[14] It's easy to build a narrative of good around plastic straw reduction, but the actual impact to the planet, and their own operational contributions to waste reduction, are negligible.

For organizations, it is crucial to work credibly and with a long-term perspective on solutions in this field and not to misuse narratives and communication for concealment and manipulation. McDonald's for instance, has now set the goal to entirely transition away from virgin fossil fuel-based plastics in their primary guest packaging to 100% renewable, recycled, or certified sources by the end of 2025.[15]

A great example of a tough but visionary decision comes from the retail pharmacy CVS Health, owner of CVS pharmacies. By 2012, the company had established mission and vision statements, but these were more textual proclamations than actionable guides. Recognizing the need to redefine and reposition itself in the healthcare sector, CVS Health embarked on a journey to crystallize its North Star narrative and reshape public perception.

The transformation began with the creation of a simple yet powerful narrative: "Helping People on Their Path to Better Health." This eight-word phrase was a distillation of CVS Health's commitment to health and wellness, serving as the North Star for future decisions and actions. This redefined purpose was not just a statement but a commitment to action, leading to the pivotal decision in 2014 to cease all tobacco sales in its then 7,600 nationwide locations. This decision, while financially impactful, was a strategic move to align the company's operations with its stated mission.

The removal of tobacco products was a risk given the potential loss in sales. However, CVS Health's commitment to its redefined purpose transcended short-term financial considerations. This bold move not only strengthened its position as a health-focused entity but also disrupted the tobacco market. A study published in the American Journal of Public Health in 2017 indicated a significant decrease in cigarette purchases in areas where CVS Pharmacy had a substantial market share. This decision not only impacted consumer behavior but also elevated the company's role in public health advocacy.

The decision to stop selling tobacco was just the beginning and it inspired employees to join the movement. They brought forward ideas for additional ways to help customers to make healthy decisions, from removing sunscreens with SPF lower than 15 from the shelves to reformulating beauty and personal care products to remove chemicals of concern.

Today, CVS Health stands as an impressive example of aligning corporate actions with purpose. Its journey from a retail pharmacy to a health-focused innovator demonstrates how a North Star narrative can lead to sustainable business growth and positive social impact.[16]

SHOWING BOLD INTERNAL AND EXTERNAL LEADERSHIP

The former Chrysler CEO Lee Iacocca was one of the world's first celebrity leaders. He joined the struggling Chrysler Corporation in 1978, saved the company from bankruptcy, and went on to revive Chrysler largely due to the introduction of the minivan. He became a celebrity after appearances in television commercials and the release of his autobiography.

Having a famous leader run a company can be both a blessing and a curse. On the one hand, they generate reach and attention for the company's messages. On the other hand, fame makes these leaders susceptible to criticism in times of crisis or when tough decisions are needed. Lee Iacocca had to learn this the hard way in 1986 after closing plants and laying off workers while simultaneously being America's highest-paid executive.[17]

Moreover, research indicates that being famous might be beneficial for executives but not so much for organizations. CEOs with high amounts of media attention receive more compensation, better protection from being fired by boards, and regular invites to join the boards of other organizations. Conversely, studies have shown that in the years following a CEO winning major media attention and awards, companies experienced negative performance trends.[18]

Great leaders in the narrative age don't focus on becoming famous for their own benefit, but they will do what's best for their organizations. They clearly understand their company's narrative North Star and moat, and they will use every opportunity to reinforce these narratives with their messaging and actions.

Another important leadership task is to create a narrative of moving boldly. Research by management consulting firm McKinsey shows that CEOs who use bold strategic moves — like productivity improvements, mergers, acquisitions, or divestitures — more than double the likelihood of rising from the middle quintiles of economic profit to the top quintile. Furthermore, CEOs who make these moves earlier in their tenure outperform those who move later, and those who do so multiple times in their tenure avoid an otherwise common decline in performance.[19]

This idea that an active CEO who moves boldly towards their organization's mission and vision is more successful is also backed by data from financial markets. When new CEOs publicly share their strategies within their first 100 days, the company's stock price can see a significant boost, according to a study from Oxford University's Saïd Business School. After analyzing over 900 public strategy presentations by new CEOs, the study found that stock prices rose by an average of 5.3 percent after such announcements. While some believe strategies should be kept internal, this research suggests that public presentations can positively impact investor perceptions by reducing uncertainty. Notably, fewer than half of the CEOs in the study made public strategy announcements in their first 200 days, indicating a missed opportunity for many.[20]

One of the boldest management decisions in the past decade was taken by Nvidia cofounder and CEO Jensen Huang. Nvidia initially created microchips called Graphics Processing Units (GPUs) to enhance video game graphics. Huang then noticed the astonishing capabilities of early AI applications in the area of image recognition and anticipated much more to come. He concluded that AI technology would revolutionize society and was even willing to bet his company on it. Greg Estes, a vice president at Nvidia, remembers, "He sent out an email on Friday evening saying everything is going to deep learning, and that we were no longer a graphics company." Success proved Huang right. In the area of AI, there is no bypassing Nvidia today, which has made the company one of the most valuable in the world.[21]

This underlines the idea of narrative constellations and their positive impact on credibility. Stakeholders will be more convinced that a company can achieve its aspirational goals if the CEO builds a narrative of bold decision-making. External stakeholders value senior leaders who are well-aligned with and passionate about their organization's mission and constantly demonstrate that they will do what it takes to get there.

Internal stakeholders are best motivated by an inspiring mission and vision that connects the organizational narratives with their personal narratives.[22]

This leadership style has been described by organizational researchers as transformational leadership and stands in contrast to classical transactional leadership, where leaders motivate their team members through rewards, recognition, or punishments based on performance.

Organizations with a clear, compelling, and inclusive North Star narrative are positioned to make their employees feel like they're part of something more meaningful. The transformational leadership theory has been extensively researched and strongly correlates to individual and organizational performance.[23]

In summary, leaders, especially CEOs, are in a prime position to communicate for their organizations because they will naturally receive the most attention from all stakeholders. They should use this opportunity to reinforce the organization's narratives, show bold leadership in striving for strategic goals, and inspire their employees to follow them on this journey.

NARRATIVE MANIPULATION: THE GOOD, THE BAD, AND THE UGLY

In 2004, a large petrol company launched a "carbon footprint" calculator for everyone to assess how much their daily life contributed to global warming. Today, the carbon footprint is a well-known concept used everywhere to remind us how we are liable for heating our planet. What is not so well known is that the carbon footprint is a narrative specifically designed to promote the idea that climate change is not the fault of oil giants but that of individuals.

While it's good to reduce personal carbon footprints, there's evidence that this term was used to shift blame away from big corporations. Case in point: Even when the 2020 pandemic saw a massive drop in individual carbon footprints due to lockdowns, the overall amount of carbon dioxide in the atmosphere (which affects global warming) hardly changed. So, even though globally we as individuals made fewer "carbon deposits" in 2020, atmospheric carbon dioxide levels still reached an all-time high.[24]

Joachim Weimann, an economist who researches the role of narratives in public discourse, argues that narratives are necessary for understanding the world, and there is no way around them. Still, there are good narratives that explain and simplify without distortion, and there are bad narratives that intend to manipulate. Then there are ugly narratives that Weimann describes as fake news, conspiracy theories, and plain old bullshit.[25] While fake news stories are lies disguised as truth and conspiracy theories sometimes claim quite complex causal relationships that could theoretically be true (Watergate was initially a conspiracy theory which later proved to be true), bullshit is simply nonsense that has no relationship to the truth.

The carbon footprint narrative would fall into the bad narrative category. It intends to manipulate and direct the conversation away from the fossil fuel producers to all of us as consumers and individuals. At the same time, the sentiment is not wrong that our efforts to strive for a cleaner world do matter. That's also the reason why the advertising campaign proved to be brilliant. Of course, no one should be shamed for declaring an intention to reduce their carbon footprint. And what's wrong with an oil giant helping all of us with a carbon footprint calculator to see and understand the issue?

Examples of ugly narratives can easily be witnessed from political actors. Russia has used systematic disinformation campaigns for years, spreading lies and false narratives. A standard narrative accompanying the invasion of Ukraine is that NATO was planning to attack Russia. Even in the ugly narrative category, a trait of incredibly successful narratives remains. Research on disinformation campaigns has shown that the most convincing Russian narratives are not total fabrications, as they contain a kernel of truth. However, this truth is only there to help these narratives better resonate with their audience's existing narrative landscape while carrying lies that exploit the divisions in societies.[26]

An example of a good narrative is the 1.5°C goal, which was agreed upon at the Paris UN Climate Conference in 2015. *The Guardian* newspaper later called this result "the world's greatest diplomatic success." The Paris Climate Deal intends to keep global warming well below 2°C and pursue efforts to limit it to 1.5°C. It's the culmination of more than 20 years of UN climate talks and led 194 parties to agree to reduce emissions and accept a goal of zero net emissions by later in the 21st century.

The 1.5°C goal is a great case study of conceptualizing an otherwise hard-to-grasp problem and uniting the whole world behind it. International climate negotiations were often marred by an absence of clear, unified targets, and they needed to find common ground between the interests of developed countries with large carbon footprints and the developing countries most vulnerable to the effects of climate change.

This seemingly simple numerical goal of 1.5°C has since become the rallying cry and a critical narrative for climate activists, policymakers, and businesses worldwide. Its widespread adoption has fostered a sense of unity and driven collective action, helping the global climate movement advance its mission of mitigating the worst impacts of climate change. In the 10 years following the agreement, invested capital for clean energy solutions accelerated significantly to 12 percent and continues to rise yearly.[27]

Narratives are powerful tools that can steer the direction of an organization's growth, reputation, and public perception. Companies can establish a strong and unique moat around their businesses by adopting and promoting good narratives. However, narratives can be used to manipulate and deliberately mislead audiences into believing in a more positive reputation than their underlying reality. This reputation-reality gap will eventually be revealed and poses a substantial risk to the trust of the most essential stakeholders.[28] Staying authentic, honest, and purposeful on the narrative journey is paramount for the long-term success of any organization.

IDEAS FOR ACTION

Building a solid reputation for an organization is a continuous journey, not a one-time project. Think of it as tending a garden; you can't just plant seeds and walk away, expecting them to grow. You need to water, nurture, and protect them regularly. Similarly, a company's reputation isn't built overnight or with a single campaign. Just like any other competitive advantage, it requires consistent effort, care, and attention. Central to this effort is the art of developing compelling narratives that resonate with your audience. It's a never-ending process of trying, failing, reflecting, and, above all, learning. Here are a few ideas to help you do that:

Listen to your audience and utilize the existing narrative landscape. Designing a narrative map with a profound understanding of the stories and narratives of your audience is the best basis for developing narratives. Don't just think about creating new narratives. Familiarity with an existing narrative can make people more open to a new narrative and make it more compelling.

Understand the difference between a narrative and a slogan. A narrative does not have to be a slogan, but a slogan can get attached to a narrative. A slogan is a short and memorable phrase used to get a narrative across in a concise and catchy way. If done well, it will bring the entire narrative to mind in just a few words. Examples of slogans are "Diamonds are Forever" from DeBeers or "Just do it" from Nike.

Great slogans are hard to find and often need time to evolve and become iconic. DeBeers initiated the engagement ring narrative in 1938. Still, the slogan "Diamonds are Forever" was only invented 10 years later by ad writer Frances Gerety who thought of it right before bed one night after forgetting to brainstorm for a meeting the next morning.[29]

Because slogans are complicated, it's advisable to mentally separate slogans from narratives. A narrative can be bulky and cumbersome in the beginning as long as it catches the essence of what you are trying to say. It can range from a few words to a longer narrative statement with a few sentences or be based on a structured approach (as we'll see in the next point). Writing it down in plain language is vital to make it easy to understand. After all, this should be the essence your audience will be able to explain in their own words if the narrative is understood and internalized.

When Elon Musk first talked about venturing into space, he most likely did not use the slogan "Making Humanity Multiplanetary" but described his vision with a couple of sentences. Such a narrative statement does not have to be explicitly communicated. It can remain an internal document that is the basis for all resulting communications initiatives that pay into the narrative.

Check your narratives for completeness and understandability. Chapter 2 described the structure of a narrative based on the model of the FrameWorks Institute and illustrated it with the Brexit example. The structure follows the three dimensions of the story world: what happens in the story, how the story is told, and how it is received. Each dimension has features like character, plot, or point of view. This structure is a great way to build your narrative statement as the source for everything else.

Use narrative constellations to increase credibility. The strategic narrative and the narrative moat should align and amplify each other. Think of the narrative landscape as the whole sky including all of the stars and constellations. The goal is to place the strategic narrative as the organization's North Star in the sky and support it with constellations of various narratives for specific stakeholders, such as customers, investors, or the public. Remember that some of these constellations can and should be about where you come from as an organization. But you should then offer a way forward by harmonizing the past, present, and future.

Don't assume that your North Star narrative is a sufficient value narrative. Smaller companies and startups might initially confuse both narratives. There are many businesses out there with long statements on their website about the purpose of the organization without providing sufficient insights into what their product or service actually does for customers. A customer wants to buy something now and cares about the value now. A future vision can be helpful, especially if it reinforces the value narrative, but it's not the key argument for customers.

Empower and inspire. It's easy to get lost in narrative definitions and lose sight of the main goal: a great narrative will empower your stakeholders to envision a brighter future for themselves with the help of your organization.

Incorporate elements of surprise or novelty to captivate and inspire. Ensure your narrative unifies rather than divides, fostering shared purpose. No matter how ambitious your future goals are, they must be realistic and align with your organization's strengths and capabilities.

Finally, assess the uniqueness of your narrative. Does it provide your organization or company with a distinct competitive advantage? Organizations must demonstrate why their existence is important and the significance they hold in the lives of their target groups. If your narrative is interchangeable with that of your competitors, it's time to develop a more distinctive one.

Now that we've completed an overview of the key narratives for organizations, it's time to roll up our sleeves and bring these narratives to life. This is where narrative strategy meets reality, and the best way to prepare for it is to expect and embrace the complexity that will likely follow.

7. BRINGING NARRATIVES TO LIFE

THE BARBENHEIMER SURPRISE

As of February 2024, *Barbie*, directed by Greta Gerwig, was on its way to $1.5 billion USD in revenues, already making it the most successful film in the history of Warner Bros. This unprecedented box office success is attributed to a meticulously planned and relentless $150 million USD marketing campaign that even outspent the estimated production cost of about $145 million USD. A vital component of the campaign was a dizzying array of partnerships. The team worked with the likes of Airbnb to design a real-life Malibu Barbie Dreamhouse through a massive pink makeover of a Malibu mansion. They even collaborated with Burger King to create a pink burger. Overall, the film promotion featured 165 brand partnerships, boosting its visibility across various sectors. The marketing team strategically targeted multiple generations, moving beyond traditional Mattel toys to include partnerships with video games, fashion retailers, and even rug manufacturers.

But one of the biggest drivers of excitement and engagement for the movie wasn't planned at all. It emerged organically on social media. On January 1st, 2023, film critic David Ehrlich tweeted:

> 7 months and 21 days until Barbenheimer

The term "Barbenheimer" referenced the simultaneous release of *Barbie* and *Oppenheimer* on July 21, 2023. The term gradually gained momentum and took off with audiences a month earlier as fans circulated thousands of memes and comments on the convergence of both films, receiving an overwhelmingly positive reception. The striking differences in aesthetics, tone, and intended demographics between the two films sparked debates over which movie to watch first, and some fans even considered the prospect of viewing both back-to-back.

The Barbenheimer phenomenon had measurable effects on the public awareness of both movies. *Barbie* received over 1.4 million online mentions on release day. *Oppenheimer*'s online mentions were around a third of *Barbie*'s, peaking at over half a million on release day. Mentions that included both *Barbie* and *Oppenheimer*, or the term "Barbenheimer," accounted for over 280,000 online mentions on release day — more than half of the total number of mentions accrued by *Oppenheimer*. The Barbenheimer discussion was embraced by the social media teams of both films and ultimately benefited both.[1]

Social media has revolutionized communication and marketing strategies, transforming them from meticulously planned sequences of events into a vibrant, multifaceted dance of actions and reactions. Today's audiences possess unprecedented power, and companies that can ignite creativity and participate in the conversation will resonate on a scale previously unimaginable.

But why do some narratives go viral and achieve widespread popularity through rapid sharing, while others fail to be picked up at all? Robert Schiller has done extensive research about economic narratives and concludes in his book *Narrative Economics* that "It is difficult to state accurately or to quantify the reason a few economic narratives go viral while most fail to do so. The answer lies in a human element that interacts with economic circumstances. Beyond some simple and predictable regularities, a network of human minds sometimes acts almost like a random number generator in selecting which narratives go viral."[2]

While virality itself cannot be planned, a great campaign can increase the odds of it happening. Warner Bros. president of global marketing Josh Goldstine explains the approach for *Barbie*: "In every campaign, there are elements of earned media like social media and paid media [such as a trailer spot]. We believe this brand had the opportunity to generate some exciting earned media. Some of the choices we made stimulated that. Then it did totally take on a life of its own."[3]

The campaign team knew earned media would contribute to much of the marketing buzz. Unlike paid advertising, earned media is not directly controlled by a company and cannot be bought directly. This meant being open to the audience's point of view and ideas and embracing them. This can still be a planned process, as Goldstine describes: "We saw it as a breadcrumb strategy, where we gave people little elements of the movie to stimulate curiosity and that created conversation."

The first breadcrumb was released at CinemaCon 2022, a large gathering of movie theater owners from around the world. "We put out a single image of Barbie in her Corvette in Barbie Land. It was one of those moments that took on a life of its own. About a month later, they were shooting in Santa Monica, and we knew people were going to be able to take pictures on the street of Margot and Ryan in their multi-color dayglow outfits on the beach. We started to see the material electrify the culture."

The breadcrumb approach also worked very well for brand partnerships. The early enthusiastic reactions from fans and the initial buzz around the movie created a huge desire for brands to become a part of the *Barbie* narrative. Goldstine again: "Brands wanted to become part of this because they saw the film was finding its way into culture in such a dynamic way. It stopped becoming a marketing campaign and took on the quality of a movement." He also adds that he had never before seen this degree of interest and brand engagement: "I've been doing this for 35 years. This is one of the most unique experiences I've ever had."

NARRATIVES ENABLE STRATEGIC IMPROVISATION

Strategic improvisation isn't about running a campaign without a strategy but rather about having a flexible strategy that can be adapted as you go along. It's a balance between the foresight of strategy and the insight of improvisation. Netflix is a great example of strategic improvisation. The rapidly changing landscape of digital streaming and content consumption continues to require constant adaptation and experimentation in order to remain dominant in the streaming-service industry. Initially starting as a DVD rental service, Netflix pivoted to streaming, quickly recognizing the potential shift in how audiences would consume media. Further improvisation happened with its foray into original content production, starting with *House of Cards*, which not only changed its business model but also disrupted the entire entertainment industry. Netflix continues to blend strategic planning and flexibility by experimenting with new formats, pricing models, and content offerings.

In modern management theory, improvisation is no longer seen as a malfunction of planning but is a suitable means of remaining operational under complex and dynamic conditions.[4] In music, the ability to improvise is a sign of great mastery and command of one's craft, and the same applies to many other areas of life, including communications and marketing. Successful improvisation requires experience, creativity, and intuition.

Narratives, in this context, serve as the ideal bridge between strategy and improvisational agility. On the strategy side, narratives allow you to state the goal of the campaign, such as how you want to change the mind of your audience and what you want them to do.

A clear strategic goal for the *Barbie* campaign was to reach an audience much broader than just those playing with Barbie dolls. Based on that goal, the team created a narrative suggesting that the film would defy audience expectations. Goldstine describes an example of this narrative with a much-discussed trailer that was supposed to challenge audience perceptions: "We did a very provocative teaser trailer and put it before *Avatar: The Way of Water* which is maybe not your first thought for a *Barbie* movie. It had music from *2001: A Space Odyssey* in an homage to the Stanley Kubrick film. We wanted to make something thought-provoking. People had preconceptions. We thought that, by shaking them, we could create a tremendous amount of curiosity."

One could even argue that "The *Barbie* movie is not what you think it is" narrative was the strategic North Star of the whole campaign. I was surprised when I learned that Ryan Gosling would play Ken and saw the first pictures of him in his flashy movie outfit. I've been a Ryan Gosling fan since seeing him in *Drive*. I would not have expected him to join the cast. The second moment of cognitive dissonance came when I watched the trailer Goldstine mentioned, which looked like a teaser for a *Star Wars* movie. The next puzzle piece in my personal narrative change was the review from a film critic who was surprised by the feminist message of the story.

All of this can be planned with a smart and bold strategic narrative that fits into the narrative landscape of the intended audience. That's the strategy part.

But narratives are equally helpful for improvisation once the campaign is running. The key strength of planned improvisation in communication and marketing campaigns is that there is no need to fully predict human behavior. As we learned from Robert Schiller, there are too many factors defining what works and what does not. The idea is to stop the planning at some point and just accept that there is a degree of randomness that can't be controlled. Instead, use the energy to measure and observe what is happening and elevate what plays into your narrative.

The Barbenheimer phenomenon was not planned, but it's easy to see that it aligns very well with *Barbie*'s strategic narrative: this movie defies expectations, moving beyond the pink and happy world of an iconic doll to challenging the audience on societal ideals and norms. If *Barbie* had been a movie for kids, we can be sure that Warner Bros. would not have embraced the Barbenheimer narrative. In fact, in Japan, the Barbenheimer narrative collided with the master narratives about the atomic bombs in Hiroshima and Nagasaki and the painful memories still felt today. The combination of both films was criticized for trivializing nuclear war, and Warner Bros. Japan even released a statement disagreeing with the alignment.[5]

Narratives help to create alignment and define the long-term strategy of a campaign while, at the same time, providing a robust frame to improvise and seize opportunities as they come. Let's dig a little deeper into best practices for both concepts.

A PLAN IS NOT A STRATEGY

The *Barbie* marketing team decided to create an unconventional teaser trailer in order to widen the movie's audience and build the expectation-defying narrative. Were they certain that this strategy would work? They were not. Goldstine admits they were concerned that the reference to *2001: A Space Odyssey* might not land with its intended audience. This simple example provides a fundamental insight into communication campaigns: strategy and planning are not the same thing. In business, many often confuse the terms "strategy" and "plan," thinking they are interchangeable when, in reality, they serve distinct purposes.

A strategy is a set of choices made on a playing field with the aim of producing a victory. While you cannot know for certain the outcome, you must start with a theory. And while you may undertake intensive research to understand the market, organizational readiness, or industry trends, at the end of the day you are putting yourself out there and stating what you believe is likely to happen. You're taking a risk. Warner Bros. decided that the playing field would not be a movie for kids or just people who played with Barbies at some point in their lives. They decided to play on a bigger field for the potential gain of a wider audience, though they risked alienating their core audience. While strategy is about defining goals with the "what" and "why," planning is about how to achieve those goals.

Plans differ from strategy in that they have a defined and knowable outcome. Once the team decided to do the teaser trailer, they could plan how to create, distribute, and budget it. This might be complicated and involve a lot of skill, but it is a lot more comfortable because the outcome is within their control.

The global expansion strategy of Netflix is another example showing the difference between strategy and planning. Netflix's strategy to become the leading streaming service worldwide was based on the theory that doing so would require a highly diverse and localized content library. As a consequence and strategic choice, Netflix invested in original local productions in various countries. To execute this strategy, Netflix planned and implemented steps such as researching local markets to understand viewer preferences, establishing production capabilities in multiple countries, and negotiating licensing agreements for local content.

The challenge for many business strategies and communication campaigns is that they claim to possess a strategy when, in truth, they've only established a plan.[6]

CREATING A THEORY OF CHANGE

As we saw in the last section, creating a strategy requires defining your field of play and the desired outcome. But you also need to understand the behaviors and attitudes that need to shift in order to reach that end goal, and how your planned activities will support the change. A well-established methodology for mapping out a strategy for communications is the theory of change (TOC). This tool emerged in the 1990s from work done by the Aspen Institute Roundtable on Community Change. Stakeholders of complex change initiatives typically look at change as a black box because the process from actions to outcomes is unknown. They initiate and plan certain activities and try to observe long-term outcomes. But often, how the change process actually unfolds inside the black box is unclear. This means there is little or no attention given to the early and mid-term changes needed to reach a longer-term goal.

Let's look at an example of a theory of change from Bavaria in Germany. Many of you have likely heard about Oktoberfest and the Bayern Munich soccer team, but Germany's largest federal state also faces some significant challenges. One of them is the slow expansion of wind energy, which is desperately needed to meet the goals of a transformation towards sustainable energy. Bavaria is doing well in solar and hydropower but lags behind in wind turbines. A key reason for the slow progress is a clash of narratives between the Bavarian government, led by Governor Markus Söder, and local communities. On the one hand, the government claims the stall is due to citizens pushing back on wind energy projects because wind turbines create noise, shadow, and light reflections. However, public acceptance of wind energy is rising and is no longer the key issue. On the other hand, mayors, as representatives of these communities, complain that it's expensive and exhausting to construct a wind turbine because of the government regulations that must be adhered to when building one. There are too many rules, and some are even contradictory.[7]

A small group of mayors decided to take action. They started an initiative to convince the government about the positive potential of wind energy for the state and get rid of the narrative about unwilling local communities as the barrier. Their campaign efforts were supported by the *Initiative Klimaneutrales Deutschland* (Initiative for a Climate-Neutral Germany). The initiative's founder and managing director, Carolin Friedemann, explains the process:

> We conducted extensive research to understand the local landscape, identify key players, and establish a robust network of contacts. Based on these insights, the initiative's primary strategy centered around building a strong coalition of local mayors and providing them with the necessary resources and communications knowledge to champion wind energy. The initiative quickly understood that a major driver for mayors was self-determination. They did not want to have wind parks built right on their doorsteps by external opportunistic project developers. They wanted to be a part of the shaping process.[8]

Based on these insights, the messaging of the campaign focused on narratives of local energies, independence, self-determination, and the opportunity to open up a long-term income source for the communities.

Says Friedemann: "Our theory of change was basically a two-step process: first, let's help to convince more mayors to join the initiative and put their name on a petition. Our goal here was 10 percent of all mayors in Bavaria. In the end, we got 432 mayors to sign the petition, which is 20 percent! The second step was to hand over the list to the Governor and convince the government that this initiative from the mayors was not a movement against the government but a great opportunity to speed up the expansion of wind energy in Bavaria together."

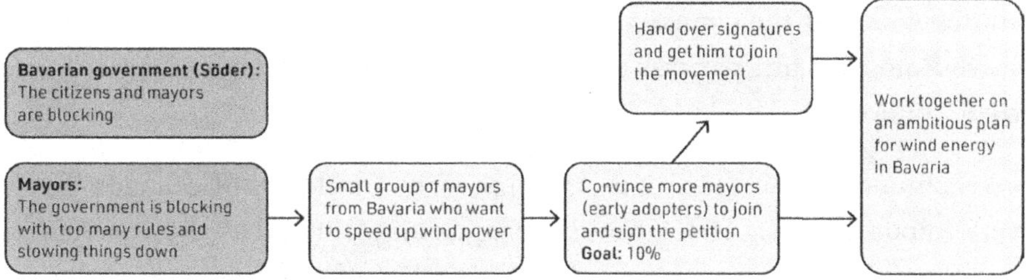

The theory of change for the wind energy campaign in Bavaria, Germany

The campaign received a lot of press coverage, especially for the official handover of signatures to Söder. He specifically said, "Thank you for this local tailwind."[9] Friedemann was happy to see how the theory of change worked out to resolve the clash of narratives but also stressed that this was not the end of the process: "Both parties continued to talk and public support by the Bavarian government for wind energy has increased — one of the core demands of the petition. The new coalition treaty signed in late 2023 also includes that the government supports remuneration for communities with third party wind turbines which was welcomed by the mayors. That's a great outcome."

Narratives are successful when they are publicly communicated and accepted, as well as when they are positively embedded in everyday communication. A sign of the discursive impact of a narrative is when key actors, such as politicians, are forced to acknowledge the rhetorical power of these narratives and can no longer participate in public debates or discussions without referring to them. The Bavarian campaign achieved precisely that. The narrative that Bavarian villages and mayors are unwilling to support wind energy is no longer an uncontested narrative. Moreover, these local authorities appear to be the driving force of change in the debate.

One reason the theory of change is so effective is the "backward mapping" or "reverse engineering" approach it employs. It starts with defining the desired long-term outcome and then working backward to identify all the preconditions necessary to achieve that outcome. This approach helps to ensure that every step in the process is directly aligned with the ultimate goal. In the case of the Bavarian initiative, the stated outcome was to change the narrative of the government. It would have been impossible to change this narrative from the outside, for example, as an environmental initiative. The strategic idea of the campaign was to build a coalition of mayors, many of them from the same party as the Minister-President, and help them to voice their opinion.

For communication campaigns, the approach of a theory of change offers a very important insight. Classic campaigns are planned based on audiences and the right messages for them. However, what is becoming more and more crucial is the sender of the message. There's too much competing information and noise in a world where everyone can become a publisher. Audiences are looking for shortcuts and signals that indicate which sources and information they can trust. Source credibility plays a major role in creating this trust. Who is actually talking to you and telling the story? The messenger is becoming the most critical factor in deciding whether to spend my time both considering and trusting the content. This fundamentally changes how communication campaigns need to be calculated.

Not everyone accepts change at the same speed. The bell curve of adopting change is a concept that describes how different people accept new ideas or changes over time. This idea is the basis for many theories of change.

Early adopters of a new narrative can become evangelists who help to get it out into the world. The effects of early adopters are amplified by social media, which makes it easy for people to participate and help spread a narrative.

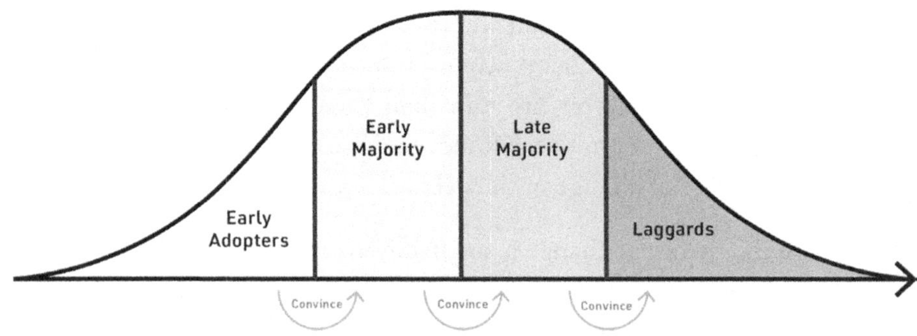

A theory of change will often align with the bell curve of adopting change, targeting early adopters first and then with their help moving on to other audiences.

"Early adopters" is a term used by technology marketers and refers to individuals who will jump at the opportunity to consume a new item (for example, DVDs, the iPhone, Bitcoin) ahead of the mass market curve. The advantage of marketing to them is that they become evangelists of a product and will do the marketing for it because they believe in it deeply. For instance, I completely ignored the release of the first iPhone in 2007, having just bought a Blackberry phone. There was one colleague on our team who would always be the first to adopt new technology, and of course he was the first of us to buy an iPhone. He took every opportunity to show us how great and easily it worked. My personal aha moment came when both of us got stuck in a huge traffic jam on the way back from a customer meeting, and we both pulled out our phones to try to find out what was going on. The small screen of the Blackberry and its press-button navigation were a world away from how easy it was to find traffic updates on the iPhone. At that very moment, Apple got me.

This influencer marketing trend is also visible in numbers. Its global market size has more than doubled since 2019. In 2023, the market was estimated at a record $21.1 billion USD.[10]

This means that before convincing your target audience, you might first have to convince a person or group of people trusted by your desired audience. Many of these influencers will only share your message if they understand it and believe in the cause behind it. The Bavarian mayors are first and foremost obligated to do what's best for their villages — they had to buy into the goal and narrative of the campaign in order to support it.

A theory of change might first include some proof points and measurable results before you can convince your full audience. An organization might first roll out a change campaign or new approach at a specific location or for a specific team and use the results and tailwind from a successful pilot for the overall rollout. This is a theory of change in action.

Even though the TOC was initially developed for complex community or social change programs, it can be utilized as a practical tool for mapping out all kinds of communication strategies. This is particularly true for narratives as they are crafted and developed over extended periods, spanning several months or even years. It is crucial not to view the entire process as a black box. Instead, it is about understanding how narrative change is expected to occur and identifying measurable milestones along the way.

The theory of change for the *Barbie* campaign used the breadcrumb approach to build early excitement and establish the narrative that "this movie is different." The initial target for these communications was fans, but even more so, potential decision-makers for brand partnerships that would help to create an unprecedented, all-pervasive presence for the actual launch campaign, reaching the early and late majority of potential moviegoers.

SEIZE OPPORTUNITIES: NEWSJACKING, AGENDA SURFING, AND DISCOURSE

In late 2019, Peloton, known for its high-end home exercise equipment, released a holiday ad that quickly became controversial. The ad featured a woman receiving a Peloton bike as a Christmas gift from her husband. Throughout the ad, she documents her year-long fitness journey. Almost immediately, the ad went viral, sparking criticism about Peloton's unhealthy depictions of body image and marriage. Many viewers perceived it as promoting unrealistic body standards, being tone-deaf, and subtly perpetuating a sexist narrative where the husband appears to be dictating his wife's fitness regime.

The controversy led to a significant discussion about gender roles, body image, and messaging in advertising. This public response negatively impacted Peloton's reputation and stock value.

But the story of the Peloton Woman wasn't over. Aviation Gin, a company co-owned by actor Ryan Reynolds, quickly capitalized on the Peloton ad controversy in a clever marketing move. They released a commercial featuring the same actress — Monica Ruiz — from the Peloton ad. The ad shows her sitting at a bar silently sipping a gin cocktail. All the while, her friends tell her she's "safe here" and "looks great, by the way." She then downs her entire drink in one gulp. The ad ends with the text "Exercise bike not included."

The Aviation Gin commercial was well-received and praised for its clever and timely response to the Peloton controversy. It's an intelligent example of newsjacking, where a brand uses a trending topic to amplify its own message.[11]

The ad's success hinged on the brand's ability to quickly produce a web commercial in nearly real-time. What is also important is that the ad resonated well with Aviation Gin's overall brand narrative. Ryan Reynolds features in many humorous ads as a stressed-out father, husband, or son who ironically reflects on topics like homeschooling or pumpkin spice season while creating gin cocktails. This sympathetic positioning and the high visibility of the brand led to the acquisition of Aviation Gin by the British alcoholic beverage company Diageo in 2020 for a staggering $610 million USD.

Newsjacking aims to capture a trending topic as it unfolds and use it to draw attention to your own content or message. The key to success is timing and relevance; the content must be current and should relate organically to the news story. Newsjacking has a high chance of gaining great visibility but also carries risks: news isn't always positive and often sparks controversy. Anyone who leverages a news story must be prepared to face criticism.

A second concept of aligning a campaign or message with a broader movement is called **agenda surfing**. Unlike newsjacking, which involves leveraging the viral nature of breaking news, agenda surfing aligns with broader, more sustained societal or political movements.

Agenda surfing means riding the wave of a theme or topic, not a piece of news, offering more time to attach and prepare one's own message to an existing discussion. Topics on the public agenda typically have a certain continuity over multiple weeks, months, or even years. Dove, a personal care brand, has successfully agenda-surfed the body positivity movement with its "Real Beauty" campaign, which celebrates natural beauty and challenges the unrealistic beauty standards set by the media and advertising industries. This campaign has positioned Dove as a brand that supports self-esteem and the empowerment of women and girls around the world.

Agenda surfing can, to an extent, be planned. As it is topic-oriented, one can monitor which topics will soon be important. Upcoming anniversaries, holidays, planned events like the Super Bowl, or trends and hype are potential opportunities for agenda surfing. It also works well for internal communications, with topics such as achieving important milestones, celebrating company or team accomplishments, or linking the internal mission and vision to external events or market news.

A third and very immediate way to seize communication opportunities is to enter into a **discourse** based on interactive feedback or questions from your audience. This insight feels obvious for many of us now, but it's worth remembering that communication was traditionally seen as a one-way persuasion tactic. Today, audiences have much more control over their sources of information, and organizations have little choice but to communicate with them on an equal footing.

An example of this comes from one of Staffbase's own customers in the automotive industry. The company in question had announced a significant change program for all of its employees which included cost savings and cutting back expenses for locations and projects.

The change program was communicated in a planned campaign with a series of articles, leadership interviews, and Q&A sessions, including town halls. Employees were highly engaged in receiving information through their employee app and intranet and heavily used comments to voice their questions and concerns. The communications team encouraged senior leaders to join the discussion, be open to feedback, and enter into a discourse about the topics. It turned out that the need for detailed information was huge. The communications team learned that no matter how many FAQs and details they shared, people still insisted on understanding why the changes were necessary and what was going to happen as a result. As questions arose, many detailed discussions emerged. This is why it's critically important to keep the conversation open and be ready to discuss changes in detail. Ultimately, these discussions will be of tremendous help to an audience that demands to understand and process change.

Leadership initially hesitated to invest time in answering questions and comments because they felt that only a small number of employees would engage in the discussion. However, diving deeper into the numbers, it was clear that though a small percentage of employees actually contributed to the discussion, there was a very high rate of employees returning to the news articles where the discussions were taking place. They came back time and again to see how the discussions had evolved and how leaders reacted to the questions and concerns posted.

Even though leaders felt they were taking part in a discussion with a small number of employees, they were in fact standing on a digital stage where many employees were looking on. The decision for leadership to enter the discussions, keep calm, share "the why" of the change, and actively engage with feedback became an essential part of the change program.

Organizations must engage in two-way dialogues to build trust and credibility. In practice, this means moving beyond the mere broadcasting of messages to actively listening and responding to the stakeholder discourse.[12]

Many leaders I talk with feel that it's easy to sit with a group of employees in a room and discuss the background to strategies and intentions. However, when it comes to conveying these intimate discussions to a broader audience, they find it more challenging. Choosing to enter into a dialogue, especially on a digital platform, is exactly that: transforming the idea of a small, closed-space, eye-level discussion into the public world. That's why this can be a powerful tool to build and double down on your narrative.

Although the predictability for all three methods varies, it's nonetheless possible to incorporate them into your planning. If significant news goes live, monitor what's going on and anticipate that you will need time and resources to react.

IDEAS FOR ACTION

Mastery is created by combining talent and hard work. The same holds true for successful narrative campaigns. Hard work means that building and establishing a narrative will take time. The goal is for the narrative to be positively adopted by your audience without the need to reenact it entirely. This effort is a marathon, not a sprint. Successful campaigns take this fact into consideration and build for the long run. This is where talent comes into play. Successful campaigns will understand the strengths of their organization, leaders, stakeholders, and the narrative landscape. The more you utilize these strengths, the more opportunities you have to stand out in the battle for attention and uniquely resonate with your audience. Here are a few ideas on how to get started.

Create signature stories: In the late 1980s, Haier, a Chinese appliance manufacturer, faced severe quality control issues, putting its reputation and survival in a competitive market at risk due to a high rate of defective refrigerators. Zhang Ruimin, appointed as the new CEO, aimed to revolutionize Haier's focus on quality and customer satisfaction. In a legendary move, Ruimin arranged 76 defective refrigerators on the factory floor and handed out sledgehammers to his employees. He led by example, smashing the first refrigerator himself, and then asked his workers to follow suit. This act was a powerful and symbolic gesture, underscoring Haier's commitment to quality and signaling to employees the critical importance of quality control and the production of reliable products. This event marked a turning point for Haier, propelling it to become today's leading global home appliance brand.[13]

The story of Haier's CEO destroying defective refrigerators is a renowned example of a signature story. These are authentic narratives that talk about turning points for an organization or individuals. Brand strategist and author David Aaker defined the concept in his book *Creating Signature Stories: Strategic Messaging That Energizes, Persuades and Inspires*. He illustrates how signature stories convey strong messages through emotional and dramatic moments. Signature stories may already exist, waiting to be uncovered and narrated effectively. In Haier's case, the CEO deliberately crafted the signature story to make a strong point about a necessary narrative shift in product quality.

Help leaders to be authentic and go the distance: Social media sets high standards and audience expectations regarding the authentic delivery of stories. This raises expectations for business leaders to deliver engaging messages and storytelling themselves rather than relying entirely on communications departments or PR agencies. Some leaders might naturally excel at speaking freely and feel comfortable with video or other interactive formats, while others may be apprehensive and try to avoid it. As an organization and communications team, finding the best format where your key messengers and leaders feel most comfortable is essential. If some are great writers, let them write; if others excel in video, use video. Warren Buffett, the legendary CEO of Berkshire Hathaway, writes the company's annual shareholder letters. Bill Gates regularly shares his thoughts on global health, development, and climate change through his blog *GatesNotes*. Many leaders, such as Mary Barra, the CEO of General Motors, use LinkedIn to provide regular updates. Choose an approach based on the leader's comfort, willingness, and ability to engage regularly, not just because it's trendy.

The same principle applies to discourse and interactive formats. Some leaders might be very comfortable in town hall or live discussion settings. In contrast, others might need more control and prefer asynchronous formats like an anonymous AMA, or Ask Management Anything, where they can have more time to prepare and consider their responses. Everyone involved should enjoy the process and even have a bit of fun along the way!

Be curious about the stories of employees and customers: Imagine a story about an employee who's been with your company for years, growing and evolving along with the business. This narrative isn't just about their professional growth but also about the passions that drive them outside of work. When you share such stories, you're celebrating their journey and highlighting the supportive and dynamic environment your company fosters. It's like telling your customers, "Look at these incredible individuals who make our brand what it is!"

The challenge is finding and elevating these stories to ensure they pay into the underlying narrative you want to build. Usually, there is not a lot of time to listen and uncover stories in our busy environments, as a common leadership trait is to be in solution mode, which expects short, analytical, and quantifiable inputs to describe a problem.

But being curious and listening or even actively asking for employee stories is worth it. Most brands struggle to find their unique and authentic way to stand out. Turning to employees is a great way to find a unique angle between your people and the organization. When employees talk about industry trends or share insights, they position your company as a thought leader, at the forefront of innovation and knowledge. It's like having an insider's guide to the industry, shared through the voices of those who navigate it every day.

Make it easy to join the narrative: Momentum is the desire to know what happens next in a story. It makes people want to hear more and leads to a desire to get involved in an issue. A great narrative is open-ended and invites the audience to continue the story through their own actions. Build momentum in a narrative by providing participatory action steps on what needs to be done or how to get involved. Ensure that action steps fit within the narrative context. Examples are joining an event, starting to research a new topic, sharing knowledge in a community, trying out a new product or service, establishing a new habit, or sharing opinions or ideas. This works even better if an audience can see themselves reflected in a narrative.

Embrace Artificial Intelligence (AI) for communications: The generative AI revolution, which started with ChatGPT in 2022, is transforming how communicators operate. Although there are concerns about AI, its potential to streamline communications work has been evident from the start. A study by Nielsen Norman Group shows that text production can become more than 50 percent faster with AI, especially by accelerating the brainstorming and drafting phase.[14] However, careful editorial oversight is needed to ensure accuracy and prevent AI from "hallucinating" and providing incorrect information.

A study by Harvard Business School examined 758 employees from Boston Consulting Group performing 18 typical tasks for consultants and found that AI significantly improved the average quality of these tasks. They also found that AI benefited the bottom half of skilled participants significantly more than the top half. This indicates that AI is particularly beneficial for those with lower skill levels, thereby leveling the playing field.[15] This is particularly relevant for large companies with many part-time communicators with limited content creation training. AI can significantly enhance their work.

The new possibilities AI creates for media are also remarkable. Images and illustrations can be created within seconds. While these may not always be directly used for communication, they provide a solid foundation for creating briefing documents for agencies or brainstorming sessions. With power comes responsibility. As AI images and voice technology are becoming indistinguishable from real humans, AI guidelines will be essential to keep the trust of your audience. For instance, we advise against using AI to create artificial images, videos, or voice recordings of employees or leaders of an organization. Another controversial aspect of AI media generation is that its results are based on the work of human artists. There's a fine line between innovation and plagiarism, undermining the value and rights of the original creators.

AI will not replace communicators, but those using AI effectively will have an advantage. Start experimenting and integrating AI capabilities into your daily work to understand its potential. Proficient use of AI will enhance creativity, improve output quality, and help to achieve more in less time.

Be prepared for a crisis: Silicon Valley Bank did not have a crisis communications plan to deal with a potential bank run. In a highly dynamic or volatile environment, it may seem like improvisation and reactive communications are the only way. This will not work in a crisis situation as events unfold too fast, and any unprepared company will be put on the defensive.

Good crisis communication planning can mitigate the risks associated with a crisis, including legal, financial, and reputational risks. It requires quick, effective responses with consistent messaging across platforms.

Best practices in this domain include thorough risk assessment and scenario planning to preempt potential crises, establishing clear communication channels for swift information dissemination, and comprehensive spokesperson training. Tailoring communication strategies to the needs of key stakeholders and developing clear, empathetic messages are also crucial. Regular training and drills are essential to keep any team well-prepared, coupled with ongoing monitoring and adaptation of strategies as situations evolve. Post-crisis, a thorough analysis is indispensable to glean insights for future improvement. This holistic approach to crisis communication steers a company through challenging times and fortifies its standing in the eyes of all its stakeholders.

Avoid over-strategizing: This is a personal insight based on my involvement in many strategic campaigns across various business areas. When finding the balance between creating a strategic plan and executing that plan while learning and adapting, I have observed that in almost all cases, too much time, energy, and effort is spent on the strategizing phase. Consequently, there isn't enough energy, endurance, and patience left to bring the strategy to life and get the desired results.

After many years in the corporate world, one of the great joys of starting with a small company is to see how fast things can move if you don't overthink them and just get started. Sure, large corporate environments encourage their members to be more risk-averse. However, always keep in mind that narrative campaigns are inherently long-term and will need time to develop. When in doubt, try to start, get your message and stories out into the world, and learn from the process. As the authors of a review project on narrative change initiatives have put it:

> Foundations are spending too much money and time on intellectually "getting it"; strategy, research, etcetera, and not enough time on experimenting and the doing of narrative.[16]

A strategy to bring narratives to life is a great foundation, but an important piece of the puzzle is still missing. People, processes, and tools need to be in place to execute the communications strategy, adapting and refining it where needed. This could easily fill a couple of books; that's why I will focus on the specific implications of a strategy on building or changing narratives.

8. ORGANIZING FOR THE NARRATIVE AGE

HOW TO REINVENT RESPONSIBILITY

Economy-class passengers on a Lufthansa flight from Riyadh, Saudi Arabia, to Frankfurt, Germany, in August 2023 had their tomato juice served by a special flight attendant: Lufthansa Airlines CEO Jens Ritter. He later shared on LinkedIn some of his key insights from the frontline experience: "I used to fly as a pilot, and so I thought I knew about the challenges a flight during the night entails. But to be present and attentive and charming — when the biological clock just tells you to sleep — was something entirely different."[1] Ritter has worked for Lufthansa for many years, but he had never before had the opportunity to be part of the cabin crew.

It's not unusual for airline CEOs to join their team on the frontline to see firsthand what's going on and to show appreciation for their hard work. For Lufthansa, the CEO's flight to Saudi Arabia was more than just a visit. It was a small piece in a much bigger puzzle intended to transform the company.

Stefanie Stotz, Head of Communications and Cultural Development at Lufthansa Airlines, explains:

> Society is changing, especially in air travel. The debate about flying and whether it still makes sense from an environmental perspective affects not only our customers but also the people who work for us. We can't just steer through the usual strategic programs to make us successful for the next few years. As a leading airline, we have to anchor the sense of purpose in our work much more strongly and become a role model for the transformation of the entire industry. Only then will we be able to position Lufthansa for the long term.[2]

Of course, Lufthansa is not alone in this challenge. As Willie Walsh, Director General of the International Air Transport Association (IATA) says: "The sustainability challenge is, bar none, the biggest that we will face as leaders of the aviation industry. This will be difficult and take time. As pioneers building the net zero emissions age for aviation, scrutiny of our efforts will be extreme. We must welcome it as a means of telling the impressive story of aviation's decarbonization and its contributions to society."[3]

In order to find the airline's new extended purpose, a Lufthansa project team conducted months of fundamental research throughout the company. Says Stotz: "The focus was on understanding where we all want to see Lufthansa Airlines in the future, but also on identifying challenges and examining our culture for strengths and weaknesses."

From all the conversations they had, the core narrative Lufthansa extracted was "responsibility." This is not surprising, as the primary concern in aviation has always been safety. A culture of responsibility ensures that every staff member, from pilots to ground crew, prioritizes safety over everything else. Responsibility has always been a strong part of the DNA of the airline, and the idea of the new North Star narrative was to think about responsibility in a broader context than before. It means extending their existing focus on flying, and as they call it, the "Born to Fly" attitude, to a more comprehensive approach: "Take Care Beyond Flying."

The Lufthansa team also found a short and memorable slogan to sum up the new narrative: “We take off to take care.” There are longer versions of the narrative, and the team even compiled a document with a full version, as well as versions that were condensed down to just 30 seconds. The shortest version reads:

> Many things have changed recently — in society, within ourselves, and in our view of the future — in which direction will we continue to develop as Lufthansa Airlines?
>
> In “we take off to take care” lies our conviction that responsibility will be the central element that makes us a leader again — something that has always been part of our DNA.
>
> Let’s think of responsibility on a larger scale than before — for our passengers, for the climate, and for the future! The most important factor for success will be to create a trusting cooperation and an environment in which every individual can effectively contribute!

From a narrative perspective, the new narrative connects to the existing strength and identity of the organization. It’s paying off that Lufthansa has invested time to ask its people about their points of view and to do research on the ground about the existing narrative landscape. Responsibility emerged as a core identity that connects everyone in the organization. The narrative change is based on an alternative narrative with an adjusted focus, with no need to counter existing beliefs. In this case, it’s a widened focus, extending the scope of responsibility beyond flying and towards becoming a leader in the transition of airline industries.

As discussed, it’s not enough to do the research and define a narrative that resonates with the existing narrative landscape. Bringing it to life in a global organization with more than 30,000 employees requires a well-thought-out theory of change, as well as structures, processes, and tools in place to make it happen. In this chapter, I want to examine four key components that are indispensable for successful narrative campaigns in a company. What’s needed are **leaders** who understand the power of communications and narratives, a **communications team** that thinks strategically, **processes** that integrate communications end-to-end, and a **platform** to reach and engage the audience and bring all the other elements to fruition.

LEADERSHIP IN THE NARRATIVE AGE

In 2023, researchers gained access to an intriguing data trove: the results of intelligence tests taken by 59,000 Swedish men, with insights about their corresponding success in the labor market later in life. The IQ assessment was conducted as part of a compulsory military conscription test and allowed the researchers to draw conclusions about whether individuals of great intelligence hold the best-paying jobs. The results were surprising: The group with the highest salaries did not necessarily coincide with the group with the highest intelligence. For those with annual salaries of up to €60,000 euros, the intelligence quotient correlated to higher income: the smarter the worker, the better paid he was. However, above this income threshold, IQ no longer corresponded with any conclusion about income level. Even more surprisingly, the top one percent of earners scored slightly worse on cognitive ability than those in the income bracket right below them.[4]

The smart, strategic leader who sits alone at the top of a company and steers the direction of thousands of employees is a myth. Organizations are increasingly recognizing this reality. A study by Harvard Business School, which analyzed job descriptions for executives between the years 2000 and 2017, shows that the demand for "social competence" increased by 30 percent, while the demand for the ability to organize finances, processes, and materials decreased by 40 percent.[5] Juggling processes and budgets intelligently is management. However, those who want to be successful today should, as leaders, be especially able to connect with people. Inspiring leaders need charisma, empathy, and enthusiasm. They need to be willing to spend the majority of their time engaging with issues that are personal to the stakeholders of the organization.

Getting more personal was also at the top of the agenda at Lufthansa after the challenging COVID-19 years and the consequences they had on the ramp-up of air travel. The pandemic posed existential challenges to airlines and forced the entire industry to undergo dramatic changes in short timeframes. This included the fast recovery it experienced following the pandemic, which put major stress on the airline system. Stotz stated: "We learned in our research that employees were craving more appreciation and dialogue. We understood that it would not be successful just to run a communications campaign and talk about the new narrative. The first step was for leaders to acknowledge the challenging times we went through and to approach employees. Before we can expect employees to follow us on the new narrative, leaders needed to change perspective and show understanding and appreciation."

This meant involving some leaders at the frontline and having them join cabin crews during their daily operations. Ritter even shared this view on LinkedIn: "Our employees were not happy with our presence — or rather the lack thereof. I think it is always a good sign when employees want to express their concerns, ideas, or even anger to their management. So we (meaning the Lufthansa Airlines board) decided to improve that! We implemented many opportunities like town hall meetings and webcasts as well as informal ones, such as summer parties or short visits to meetings that take place anyway. We offer a chat, provide information, or answer questions. Do we succeed? I hope. But we will find out!"[6]

Supporting this dialogue is one of the key topics on the agenda of the communications team. Stotz explains: "We have created a special team focused on dialogue communication. Relationship work is important, and it works best in real encounters instead of digital channels. I personally am involved in the board meetings on a bi-weekly basis and have a fixed slot for communication. We plan the dialogue formats and maintain an overall view to coordinate and ensure that they collectively present a unified image. Our goal as a communications team is to make sure all the messaging is aligned around the core narratives that we've defined."

But social skills don't just make employees feel more appreciated. They also enable leaders to lead more effectively in complex and uncertain situations. To understand this, let's take a step back and look at a strategy model from the Boston Consulting Group for defining strategies in changing environments.

The strategy experts argue in their research entitled "Your Strategy Needs a Strategy" that many executives are still relying on strategies suited for stable environments when operating in volatile and unpredictable ones. They suggest considering two key dimensions to categorize strategic planning styles. These dimensions are predictability and malleability. Predictability is about how far into the future and with what level of accuracy a company can forecast elements like demand, corporate performance, competitive dynamics, and market expectations. Malleability measures the extent to which a company or its competitors can influence market factors. High malleability means that the players in the market can significantly shape or alter the industry landscape through their actions, innovations, or strategies.

These two dimensions create a matrix that helps identify the most suitable strategic style (classical, adaptive, shaping, or visionary) for a company based on the characteristics of its operating environment.

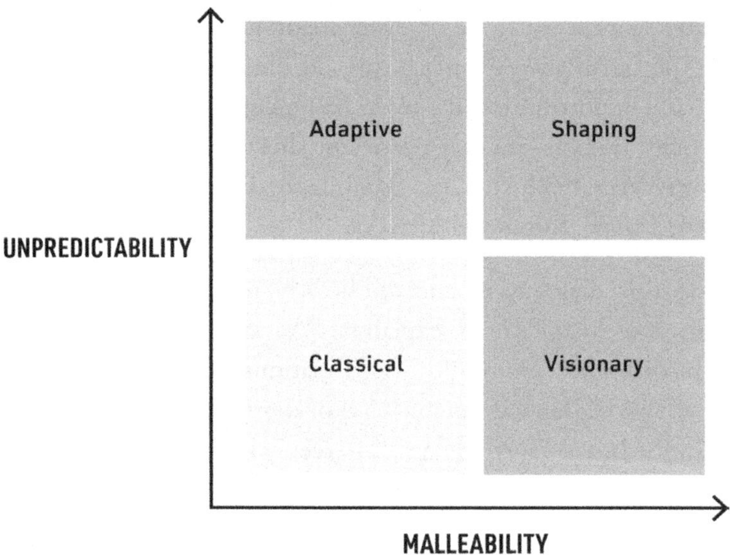

The classical style applies to mature industries in stable markets such as oil companies. Classical strategic planning can work well in this case as things move slowly enough to allow for information to pass between departments and hierarchical structures.

For the other three styles, especially adaptive and visionary, organizations need to be much more flexible with their strategic planning. They need a more agile approach whereby goals and tactics can constantly be refined. In such a fast-moving, reactive environment, when predictions are likely to be wrong and long-term plans are essentially useless, the goal cannot be to optimize for efficiency; rather, it must be to engineer flexibility.[7]

Engineering flexibility requires a clearly defined North Star narrative to help employees make decisions faster and closer to the problem instead of having to ask for permission and authority from higher levels in the hierarchy. To repeat the words of Steve Jobs: "The greatest people are self-managing ... once they know what to do, they'll go figure out how to do it ... what they need is a common vision ... leadership is about having a vision, being able to articulate that so the people around you can understand it."

What does all this have to do with cultural change, especially from the leadership perspective? Using a strong North Star narrative to align an organization behind a common vision will only work if employees feel empowered to passionately do what it takes to bring it to life. Low trust, inflexible control mechanisms, lack of ownership, or low psychological safety will all lead to lower engagement and a "not my responsibility" attitude.

Daniel Coyle shares three key skills of high-performing teams in his book *The Culture Code*. The third skill is to establish a **purpose**, which in the context of his work can be equated with a North Star narrative. However, for a purpose to take root, a team first needs to build two other things: **safety** and **vulnerability**. Safety generates bonds of belonging and identity and being vulnerable creates trust and much higher levels of cooperation.[8]

This is why the Lufthansa team decided to combine the rollout of the new North Star narrative with a cultural transformation. Stotz stated: "We have integrated the topic of Cultural Development as an essential part of communication. This means that in addition to the classic news and stories, cultural development is now part of the tasks of the communication team."

The cultural journey has received a lot of attention and engagement from Lufthansa employees. As CEO Jens Ritter explained on LinkedIn:

> A few weeks ago, I shared that all Lufthansa Airlines managers are on a cultural journey. I mentioned that one of our intended changes is creating an environment in which employees feel psychologically safe. I got so much feedback on that thought — on LinkedIn as well as offline. So let me explain a little further.
>
> The prerequisite of this is trust. And this starts with us managers. Because if everyone experiences being trusted and protected, if

> their voices are welcome, they speak up and they dare to be just like they are. In that case, employees are not afraid of making mistakes because they can simply communicate if they failed at something. As always in life, it starts with yourself. Are you authentic and approachable — do you show your real self? Do you talk about your emotions as well as your KPIs?[9]

Another great example of culture change being at the core of a company's turnaround is Microsoft. Satya Nadella took charge of the company as only its third ever CEO, following Bill Gates and Steve Ballmer. He inherited a struggling company with tired and frustrated employees. They were fed up with losing and falling behind despite their grand plans and great ideas.

Nadella describes the Microsoft culture back then: "Our culture had been rigid. Each employee had to prove to everyone that he or she knew it all and was the smartest person in the room … If a senior leader wanted to tap the energy and creativity of someone lower down in the organization, she or he needed to invite that person's boss, and so on. Hierarchy and pecking order had taken control, and spontaneity and creativity had suffered as a result."[10]

Nadella changed the company's North Star narrative to focus on leading the shift to cloud computing for all businesses, or in his own words, "Cloud computing is foundational to enabling digital transformation for any organization." This strategy has proven to be a highly successful direction, as he increased the company's value nearly tenfold from 2014 to 2024. From the beginning, the cultural shift from being "know-it-alls" to "learn-it-alls" was one of the top priorities to support and empower the rollout of the new narrative. Nadella explains: "I like to think that the C in CEO stands for culture. The CEO is the curator of an organization's culture … anything is possible for a company when its culture is about listening, learning, and harnessing individual passions and talents to the company's mission. Creating that kind of culture is my chief job as CEO."[11]

THE EVOLUTION OF THE COMMUNICATIONS FUNCTION

> *Similar to the HR function a decade ago, the communications function has the opportunity to shift to a true business partner. Those that succeed will seize this opportunity. — The Edelman Future of Corporate Communications Study*[12]

Narratives build reputation, and a key insight in studying narrative strategy is that they are all interconnected. One of the most damaging factors for the reputation of an organization is conflicting and contradictory stories and narratives. For instance, Uber claimed to be an innovative and progressive company but faced allegations of discrimination and fostering a toxic work culture, clashing with its forward-thinking narrative. Management errors need to be addressed, but it's equally important to build trust with stakeholders by showing accountability and driving consistent narratives across all audiences. This makes a strong case for an integrated communications team that owns the narrative strategy and closely coordinates with departments like HR, Finance, and Marketing. Here are some considerations for the structure of a modern corporate communications function:

Communication shifts from a cost center to a value creator. The importance of communication for companies has continuously increased over the decades, especially within the last years. COVID-19 acted as an additional catalyst, underscoring the need for timely, transparent, and empathetic messaging to maintain trust and engagement with all stakeholders. Still, many communication leaders have voiced their frustration about the constant struggle to secure sufficient resources and gain a "seat at the table," ensuring that the communications perspective is influencing important business decisions, rather than coming across as an afterthought.

Sales owns revenue. Marketing owns the pipeline and the product brand. HR owns hiring, learning, and development. Finance owns the budget. Communications should aspire to fully own reputation and the corporate brand. Committing to the responsibility for a key asset of business value creation significantly raises the profile and perceived impact of the communications function.

Communications takes ownership of building reputation and culture from the inside out. Taking full ownership of reputation goes beyond external communication and includes internal communications, helping to align employees with the company's vision, mission, and goals. As we have seen in the Lufthansa example, this can even involve the ownership of or influence over key cultural initiatives. After all, culture results from the identity of a company and its employees and is primarily formed by the existing narratives of "how we do things around here" in an organization. The core competence needed to change culture-defining narratives is found in the communications team.

Communications aligns closely with HR to build a great employee experience. There are discussions about whether internal communications should be a part of Human Resources, as quite a few communications initiatives, such as benefits enrollment and career development, are initiated by HR. There is also the emerging concept of employee experience, which aims to optimize how employees experience various touchpoints in an organization, from hiring and onboarding to professional development and offboarding. For smaller companies, HR can fully own employee relations, as there might not even be a dedicated communications team. With increasing size, complexity, and volume of messaging, the need for a dedicated communications function becomes more urgent. In this environment, internal and external communications need to be as closely aligned as possible. Every internal comms manager's nightmare is to see critical news impacting employees first on external channels without any internal heads-up beforehand. These incidents destroy employee trust and put leaders and the comms team on the defensive right from the start of critical change initiatives.

Communication has become a highly specialized skill. Another reason for centralizing communication roles is that the work is becoming a much more specialized function, requiring the skillset to understand narratives, storytelling, data-driven audience insights, and the coaching of leaders and corporate influencers. Communications has a strong career path, and while communication functions like internal, external, or investor relations have different audiences, they share similar work and skills and can greatly benefit from each other.

Communications owns the corporate brand and overall narrative strategy. A communications lead from one of the major automotive brands recently told me about the fundamental shift they are noticing in customer perceptions. The launch of a new model was traditionally a major event in their marketing strategy, and where most of the resources and budget would go. However, the company recognized from customer feedback and behavior that the focus was shifting. The key question for their audience went from "Which car should I buy?" to "Should I still buy a combustion vehicle?" or even "Should I own a car at all?"

This shift doesn't just affect the automotive sector but every industry that creates carbon emissions or causes an unsustainable use of the Earth's resources. Companies need to rethink their overall reputation and the public perception of their brand. The value narrative owned by Marketing is still highly relevant and important, but the buying decision will increasingly depend on the perception of the overall corporate brand or even a perception of the industry as a whole.

Organizations need to recognize this shift and understand how to set up the lines of responsibility between Communications and Marketing. The North Star narrative and the narrative moat become more important, and they need to be managed actively with an overarching strategy. Corporate brands can no longer choose to be invisible, taking a backseat to their product brands.

Mary Lynn Carver, a Chief Communications Officer at General Mills who was responsible for the corporate brand, said, "When I arrived at General Mills, we were a classic 'house of brands,' with no investment in the master brand. Yet there are some jobs only the corporate brand can do and that the product brands cannot do, such as taking stands on social issues. And the corporate brand uniquely expresses our purpose: 'We serve the world by making food people love.'" The Page Society has found in their research about the role of CCOs that 66 percent of them already report being responsible for the corporate brand.[13]

Communications will show up more and more at the C-suite. Traditional communication, previously seen as an afterthought and a reactive function with occasional increased visibility during crisis management, has become outdated. Modern understanding has shifted the role of communications to be proactive, anticipatory, and fundamental to both brand and operational success. This shift has implications for career paths and it raises the question of whether there should be a role for communications at the board level.

Katie Simpson is Head of Corporate Affairs and Sustainability at Hanson Search, a headhunter for top-level communications roles. In her experience, it's increasingly common that top candidates opt out of potential roles if employers don't recognize the increased importance of communications:

> The "Director of Communications" title is commonly thought of as the most senior role of its kind, but candidates are becoming increasingly aware of what this enables — and prohibits — them from achieving ... An increasing number of senior talent are opting out of Director roles when they know that's where progression caps. When the potential for your development ends just before C-Suite, and requires more firefighting than strategic, informed decision-making.[14]

The extended role of communications needs to attract the best talent in the space with great career opportunities. Increasing the impact of communications begins by acknowledging its value and potential. And that means introducing communications into the C-suite with the Chief Communications Officer.

But change doesn't stop with new roles and responsibilities for communications. There is also a major shift on the process side needed to keep pace with the speed and complexity of the narrative age.

CHANGING THE PROCESS FROM CHANNELS TO NARRATIVES

Traditional communications are organized based on key distribution channels and audiences. For instance, a function like Public Relations (PR) primarily pitches stories to the media, while Investor Relations focuses on shareholders. Social Media targets social media platforms, Internal Communications engages employees via the intranet or a newsletter, and Public Affairs concentrates on government relations. While these departments can develop a great focus and specialization, they also create silos. This leads to redundancies in content creation, conflicting messages, and missing impact, as stories will lack the focus that reinforces the key narratives. In addition, as we have seen in Chapter 7, running a communications campaign requires strategic improvisation now more than ever. This means communications organizations, and their processes, need to become much more agile and flexible in order to keep up with the pace, anticipate challenges, and utilize opportunities to promote their narratives.

For these reasons, organizations like Lufthansa and many others have adopted a more modern and agile approach called "topic-based strategic communications" or the "corporate newsroom." This approach puts content at the center of every communication effort and follows the guideline "content first, channel second." It acts like an integrated communications hub, uniting communication disciplines such as internal and external corporate communication into one organizational unit.[15]

This model often uses the term "core topic" or simply "topic" instead of "narrative." It's important to be more specific here. Topics might only be categories of stories. For instance, a company might use the topic "sustainability" to group all stories and information it releases in connection with this topic. However, there may be no underlying narrative about what exactly an audience should understand about the company's sustainability efforts. Instead, the topic becomes a random catch basin for everything and nothing. Focusing solely on topics lacks the strategy and direction needed to inspire a specific narrative in the minds of an audience. Therefore, communications teams should be highly aware of the distinction between topics and narratives, prioritizing the latter in their strategy.

Having a company strategy is essential for creating a communication strategy. This includes a vision, mission, values, and more concrete business goals. Keep in mind that a communication strategy should not just be about short-term company goals, as it takes time to build powerful narratives. An example for Lufthansa could look like this:

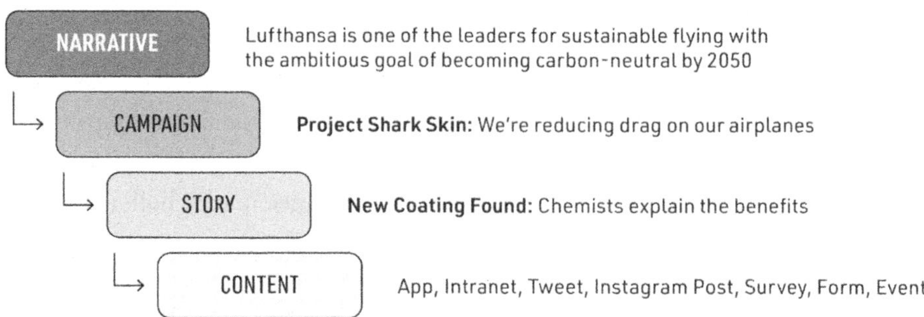

Project Shark Skin is about a bionic adhesive film applied to the surface of aircraft. It replicates the skin of sharks to optimize airflow and thus reduce fuel consumption. A campaign about the details of this new technology builds a narrative about green innovation in the airline industry, contributing to the top level sustainability narrative. The campaign consists of individual stories, and depending on the channel and audience, these stories may have specific content messages, media elements, and layouts.

Top-level narratives are ideally defined and developed with a horizon of multiple years and should have a direct impact on an important reputational dimension of an organization. Individual campaigns build more specific narratives that fill these top-level narratives with life and credibility. Campaigns rely on individual stories with specific characters, plots, and settings. These stories will comprise different content elements like a video or a news post.

A major advantage of this strategy is that it creates focus and the license for communications teams to say no. If content ideas or stories don't fit the narrative strategy, then no resources should be spent on them. A Staffbase customer from the transportation sector shared with us that this approach led them to reject more than 70 percent of content requests to their team because they were simply not playing into any of the key narratives that mattered for the organization.

The underlying structure for the strategic communications or corporate newsroom approach is a separation of narrative owners and channel owners. Narrative owners, who specialize in the content side of things, need to establish close relationships with everyone inside and outside the organization who can help to source the best information and stories for developing the narrative. On the other hand, there are channel owners who specialize in the communication channels and the specific needs and expectations of their audiences. A narrative is no longer prepared for a specific channel but stands on its own and is adapted to the required channels and specific media formats. An editor-in-chief coordinates between the narrative desks and the channel desks. In addition, other roles are conceivable, such as those for monitoring, data analysis, or content production.

A newsroom will function effectively only if there is a high level of transparency among all team members and stakeholders. It is essential for everyone to be involved and informed about ongoing projects. Meetings are central to coordination efforts. Meeting only once every two weeks is insufficient; daily meetings, even if brief, are necessary. Regular standup meetings can address questions such as: What is the current resonance of our campaigns? What are the opportunities that we previously overlooked? Where do we need to adjust our messaging to align more effectively with existing narratives?

In meetings, employees with diverse expertise collaborate, setting aside their hierarchical positions to collectively create narratives and stories and to synchronize their communication strategies. Frequently, the project team responsible for a task makes decisions rather than a senior manager.

The open and transparent approach is significantly enhanced by the right work environment. Open workspaces, in contrast to individual offices, promote the unimpeded exchange of information and encourage interactions among employees. Numerous leading companies have modified their spaces to support this model, either by dismantling walls or by creating new areas specifically designed for a corporate newsroom environment. The COVID pandemic demonstrated that this setup can also function effectively in a completely virtual format. As with many other collaborative team endeavors, the benefits and challenges of remote work are also relevant in this context.

As an organization grows in size, its need for digital tools for planning, production, and distribution also increases. While there are inexpensive or even free tools available for initial use, they may not suffice for larger organizations that have more complex demands and a greater number of stakeholders. Let's explore the rapidly expanding space of communication tools, collectively known as CommTech, in more detail.

THE RISE OF COMMTECH

Communications teams often look enviously at their marketing colleagues. Marketing has undergone a significant transformation in recent years and is now more data-driven than ever before. Marketers can connect their activities across every stage of the funnel to outcomes with the goal of turning a target audience into prospects, customers, and ultimately fans of a brand. Marketing has access to more and better data about their impact and contribution to the business goals, and money and resources are allocated where a return on investment is clearly established.

But what exactly is MarTech, and what can communications learn from it? When we founded Staffbase, I was the closest to being a marketer in our founding team. I have a marketing degree and I already had a lot of experience in content marketing activities. However, I had never before been completely in charge of marketing at a company. Being at a startup is all about stepping out of your comfort zone, so I was more than happy to take on this challenge. Staffbase started right away to market our first product — the employee app — to an international audience, which meant that we had significant needs for technology in marketing.

We needed a website, a blog, targeted emails, an email newsletter, a webinar tool, a Customer Relationship Management (CRM) system to track leads, a way to measure analytics across all tools, and a means to automate certain processes. We started off scrappy by using cheaper, open-source tools to keep costs low. I soon found myself spending a lot of time connecting tools and doing a lot of manual work to gather data and understand where leads were coming from. We knew that there was software out there that could integrate all these individual tools into a single platform. One of the main players in the market was HubSpot, based in Boston, and now one of the market leaders for marketing automation platforms. It took us quite a long time to decide on HubSpot because, after all, it was expensive. However, at a certain point, our frustration with all these tools was significant enough to push us to make the decision.

From the moment we introduced HubSpot, I had for the very first time data that connected the activities we did with the results we saw. For instance, it helped me to understand that we should double down on blog articles, because it was our quality content that prospects found on Google that was driving most of our initial demo requests for Staffbase.

An integrated marketing platform helps connect the dots and leads to crucial insights about which actions produce which types of results. Moreover, software designed for specific roles and tasks is highly empowering because it integrates many best practices and lessons learned. By introducing the new platform, I became a better marketer. For the first time, I had dashboards that I could show to our team and our investors. I was a beginner in many marketing disciplines but, using specialized software, I could now navigate the steep learning curve with the best minds in the industry helping me do my job.

What helped me get up to speed as a marketer for a young company has transformed an entire function. John Iwata, formerly CMO of IBM, remembers living through the digitalization of marketing: "As I compared notes with fellow CMOs during that time, I found that we were all doing the same thing: Heavily investing in technology, new job roles, changing processes, reskilling our people, reskilling ourselves. This was generally known as 'MarTech.' And today, you cannot be a modern marketer without mastery of MarTech."

Iwata went on to chair a research working group about the emerging role of the Chief Communications Officer for the Arthur W. Page Society, a global professional association for senior communication leaders. It was in this context in 2019 that a new term was coined. Iwata remembers: "At some point in our deliberations in the formation of the Page report, Rob Flaherty, then chairman of Ketchum, asked: 'Everyone in marketing understands MarTech. Where's CommTech?' We latched onto that as a term to describe the digital transformation of communications."[16]

Why did MarTech develop much faster than CommTech? Understanding the answer to this question can help communicators develop a better grasp of where to follow MarTech as a role model and where to deliberately deviate.

Customers are a decisive stakeholder group because they ultimately determine the success or failure of a company. Whatever drives revenue will capture the attention of the leadership. Marketing employs clear calls to action (CTAs) that help build a buying journey. For example, at Staffbase, our goal was to get people to read our blog posts and engage with them on social media. The next step would be downloading content such as a white paper or joining a webinar. Once interest was generated, prospects would visit our website and request a demo, usually marking the first direct one-on-one interaction with a prospect. At this point, a handover to sales would occur, with marketing having completed most of its job. The systematic use of a CTA represents a disruptive change in the realm of marketing technology. For communications, CTAs are not the norm but the exception. Some specific campaigns, like participation in an event, completing the annual employee survey, or getting talent to apply for a job, lead to specific CTAs, but much of today's communications operate at the awareness level without a clear goal of a stakeholder journey in mind.

With the rise of digital technology, marketing was able to shift from measurement to attribution. It's one thing to measure the likes on a social media post, but attribution has made it possible to directly link the social media post to a conversion or a sale. This empowers marketing to better predict the return on invested capital in the pipeline. However, marketers face tough challenges in the future as major platform owners like Apple or Google drastically tighten privacy rules, for instance by banning third-party cookies and increasing link tracking protection. This means marketing will have much more limited insight. Marketing experts like Rand Fishkin, the founder of the marketing audience research tool SparkToro, already talk about the "end of attribution."[17] So, the marketing lead on the measurement side will fade; communications should take this as an inspiration to close the gap even more and make measurement a top priority.

Every key-player in the C-suite has a system of record to help them understand and prove their impact in relation to the resources they invest.

Communications will have to embrace the same level of professionalization to reach and engage their audience with communication and prove its impact.

This is also a key component of the Lufthansa strategy, as Stotz points out: "Narrative campaigns can only be effective when people can truly experience and participate in them. What's needed is an architecture to reach and especially engage the audience and bring everything together."

This is what drives us at Staffbase: to build the leading CommTech platform for the narrative age. But this emerging category is not just about us — many other vendors are in the market driving this change. My intention at this point is not to discuss specific tools or features but to provide a few core priorities that will become defining for CommTech platforms:

From tools to platform: As previously described, a major innovation of digital technology in marketing was linking cause and effect. This can only work if a function doesn't rely on multiple individual tools. Yes, in theory, they all could be connected, but the technical expertise and understanding required are substantial, and in reality, it will not happen.

The goal of a communications platform should be to support an end-to-end process, from creating the communications strategy and making it transparent for all involved departments, to operational planning detailing what will happen and when, to the actual creation and distribution of content to key audiences, and the management of reactions and interactions. All these activities will yield insights that demonstrate what works and how all this positively impacts key narratives, reputation, and, ultimately, business results.

Multichannel support: Talking about communications and multiple channels is tricky. Why? Whenever we ask communicators if they want more channels, they typically say no because more channels means more complexity and more effort. This is true now, because each channel in their world is a new tool that needs to be integrated. Or worse yet, it never gets integrated and just increases the amount of work to fill it with content and get any feedback and analytics out of it. In that regard, having more channels is bad.

However, from an audience perspective, it's great to have channels to adopt that fit well with their work profile. After all, this is what marketing embraced many years ago to the point that omnichannel marketing concepts are now the undisputed standard for reaching an audience at the right time in the right channel, and with the right message. If we take a look at an example from employee communications, modern intranets are a channel that works pretty well for a workforce that is mostly desk-based, while employee apps are effective for frontline workers or anyone else on the go. Email newsletters are suitable for busy individuals like salespeople or leaders who want the most important information delivered in as condensed a format as possible.

The rising importance of employee communications, supported by the fact that reputation is built from within, means that the channel mix needs to include both internal and external channels. Some channels might be exclusive to one audience or the other, while others might be used for both. For instance, LinkedIn has become an important channel for both internal and external communications. Many leaders use LinkedIn specifically to reach both audiences, and most communications teams will want to integrate LinkedIn into their overall channel mix. So, the goal should not be to have fewer channels. Instead, focus on having the channels you need to reach your audience. At the same time, having just one platform simplifies and automates the management of channels and consolidates the results in one place.

Narratives play a key role in the platform. The lack of awareness about the power of narratives and their distinctiveness from stories has resulted in their virtual nonexistence in current communication technology platforms. Communicators need to do a better job of educating their leadership teams on the importance of narratives and the narrative strategy that will establish a clear direction, akin to a guiding North Star, and the narrative moat for the business. Narratives bridge the gap between the awareness generated by communication metrics such as likes, clicks, and views, and tangible business results such as reputation measurement. Introducing narratives at a platform level allows communicators to receive regular updates on their progress. In this regard, narratives should be viewed as calls to action. As discussed in Chapter 2, narratives can be measured because they are meant to build an opinion in the audience's mind, and it's often possible to specifically ask for this opinion.

For example, Lufthansa conducts a yearly anonymous questionnaire for its employees to assess their satisfaction with working at the company. This survey is known as "Involve Me!" As part of the cultural change initiative, employees are also asked about their feelings towards the efforts to change the company culture. These insights will be used to learn about the impact of the culture change activities underway.

And while yearly surveys are good, many communications teams would love to have more frequent check-ins to measure progress and understand how they can fine tune their campaigns. One challenge with surveys though is the abundance of them today, leading to a certain survey fatigue among audiences. However, through tests on our own platform, we have learned that a pulse check can be very effective when administered at the moment of information consumption. This means that a simple question related to the narrative can be regularly incorporated as part of the information encountered by the audience. This allows for continual check-ins on the progress of the narrative coming to life. We implemented this functionality on the Staffbase platform and call it Smart Impact. Using in-the-moment pulse checks, communicators can track the effects of their efforts to progress a narrative in the hearts and minds of employees.

Artificial Intelligence (AI) will play a significant role in CommTech. AI will be so important that I will use two points to describe its impact. The first point is about the upsides and positive effects of AI. Since the launch of ChatGPT, it has become evident that AI helps in creating content faster and in higher quality, including idea generation, drafting, and review of content. This also increasingly involves the creation and improvement of media such as pictures, videos, and voice recordings. For instance, tools like HeyGen allow the translation of a video from a speech into another language with the same voice as the original speaker including the automated lip sync of the voice track. It feels like magic and can surely be a powerful tool to reach more audiences with important messages. We can expect a world of innovation in this space, which will either result in specific tools used by communicators or be integrated into larger CommTech platforms.

Another area that will benefit from AI is the analysis of communication results, especially in searching for patterns and learnings based on data. AI will also allow these insights to be summarized in a more accessible way for different kinds of audiences.

A potentially high-impact use case will be to combine the insights of this book with the capabilities of AI. Narratives, as a new and powerful focus for communications, can help craft better messages that resonate more effectively with the existing narrative maps of an audience. AI can help build and evolve narrative maps and automatically align a narrative strategy with all the messages that a large communications organization sends out. AI will also assist in measuring the distribution of narratives and extracting narratives from existing data.

One concrete idea we are exploring is the ability to simulate how people will react to a message before it's even sent. Every communicator knows that feeling: You've got your message polished, your team's on board, and you're ready to reach out to lots of different people. The key is to avoid surprises, craft the perfect message, and be ready for whatever comes next — be it questions or any other kind of feedback. AI enables the alignment of the key narratives of the message and the overall campaign with the narrative maps of your key audiences. Before your message ever goes out, you get a clear picture of what might need tweaking. AI, and specifically the capabilities of large language models, seem perfectly suited for the narrative age.

CommTech plays a crucial role in mitigating the risks of AI. More so than many technologies which have come before, we are all aware of AI's incredible potential and, simultaneously, the potential for its misuse, such as being a tool for creating fake news and spreading lies. CommTech will be key in building and maintaining trust with an audience in various ways. One of the most critical is the rising importance of channels and the branding of them to build an audience's trust. In an era when content like AI-generated pictures become increasingly perfected, making it almost impossible to distinguish what is fact and what is fake, the channel becomes the key instrument to verify whether the information is from a credible, official source or if it's part of a disinformation campaign. This means it will be critical for organizations to have a clear channel branding strategy and develop strong, owned channels to control the distribution of information, especially in times of crisis.

A second contribution of CommTech solutions in the era of AI is to provide ongoing screening and early detection systems in the information space to identify potential challenges or upcoming crises as early as possible. Looking further into the future, we could also envision things like automated correction bots which help counter misinformation by understanding the context and providing links to credible sources of information. We can then imagine a world where we don't just see automated and highly targeted disinformation campaigns like we have today, but also the same level of technological advancement on the side of fact-checking and challenging fake news to ensure authentic stories prevail.

EPILOGUE

In October 2023, as I was nearing the completion of the first draft of this book, I received a call from a friend. She coordinates a group of companies that are pushing for a faster expansion of renewable energy in the region. In fact, their goal is to become one of the lighthouse projects in Germany for building green hydrogen infrastructure.

These companies, rooted in the manufacturing industry, face a significant challenge: their production processes consume vast amounts of energy, making the development of cost-effective, long-term options for a sustainable energy supply critically important. The plant managers were well aware of this challenge. They had worked out a plan to collaboratively spearhead the adoption of a new, green infrastructure. However, they needed buy-in from additional stakeholders. Political involvement was essential to secure financial support and gain quick project approval. The overall combined workforce of more than 5,000 employees needed to be convinced, as this long-term project would bring many changes. The employees could also serve as ambassadors for this initiative in the region since they are connected to associations and communities and with family and friends.

The team knew this would require a good communication plan. What they didn't anticipate was just how daunting and complex that communications effort would be. Their arguments for addressing climate change with renewable energy were met with skepticism. In some cases, they could not even agree on the basic facts — for instance, that climate change is real and that collective action towards sustainable energy sources is needed. The group was well prepared to explain their plans and the way in which all the technical details would work. They were ready to address the how, not the why, and even more importantly, not the why for each stakeholder group.

That's when she called me. She asked if I could facilitate a workshop to refine their communication strategy. I was happy to support them but was not sure how I could be most helpful in this case. Had this request come a year earlier, I would have suggested sitting down and reviewing and improving their current messaging together. Yet, the journey of writing this book had shifted my perspective. I approached the workshop with a novel strategy in mind. Rather than focusing on crafting specific messages, I aimed to empower them to rethink their approach through the lens of narrative building. How could they first find a common basis and then build a narrative that would resonate with the narrative map of their audiences? It was a shift from "how to communicate" to "how to think about communication."

We conducted the workshop and discussed the topics you've encountered in this book. We explored what a story is and how a narrative is different and more powerful. We had them define what are the key narratives for their audiences and specify which of them are contention points and which could be common ground. We asked ourselves what a message would need to look like to resonate with their key stakeholders. We highlighted existing narratives they would need to change, and discussed whether they should change them through counternarratives or alternative narratives. I needed about 45 minutes to lay out the basic concepts, and based on that, we began discussing ideas for their specific case.

As mentioned, I've facilitated countless communication workshops throughout my career, and yet I've rarely witnessed a group experience as many aha moments as this one. Previously, communication seemed to them like a black box — something for which they would always need expert help to craft better messages. However, introducing them to the narrative framework opened the box. They suddenly felt empowered and able to comprehend the cause and effect of their messaging with great clarity.

A prime example of this newfound understanding was their initial reluctance to use the term "Heimat," a German word that conveys a profound sense of home and embodies a deep narrative about belonging. The challenge with the word is that it has been appropriated by far-right groups to promote a nationalist and exclusionary view of identity and belonging. However, the original meaning of the term is a very positive, personal, and emotional connection to place and community without exclusionary or ideological overtones. Through our discussions, they came to see "Heimat" not merely as a word but as a narrative deeply ingrained in all of us. It became recognized as a universal desire for a place where we belong and which has contributed to building our personal identities.

As we have learned in this book, changes need to be grounded in our existing reality — in the here and now. The transition towards a carbon-neutral society will be a significant change for all of us in the decades to come. We need to connect this change to our identity, to make it both part of who we are and where we are going. That's why we should not let a powerful term like "Heimat" be taken away from us.

The workshop's feedback was overwhelmingly positive. Participants expressed astonishment at how manageable communication suddenly seemed and how they now had a clear direction for moving forward. Remarkably, as a collective, they began to generate arguments and ideas far surpassing any I had previously conceived for their situation.

For me, the workshop underscored the transformative potential of the narrative framework to teach people the skills to sustain themselves over simply providing them with their immediate needs. This shift from creating messages and content to empowering others is a goal of every advanced communications team I have met. However, equipping leaders and line managers with better communication skills is challenging — how exactly do you teach this to somebody? The most common approach is to share comprehensive briefing documents with key messages for the most important initiatives.

Now, instead of just telling leaders what exactly to say, explain the narrative you want them to align with. A narrative is much easier to remember, but more importantly, leaders can use their own creativity, authenticity, and stories to help bring the narrative to life. The methodology in this book is not just an addition to the process of becoming better strategic communicators; it's a transformative way to empower inspiring leaders. With that, I wish you the best of luck in your communications endeavors.

ACKNOWLEDGEMENTS

Writing this book was a team effort. As the cofounder of a fast-growing global company, it has been a luxury to be able to follow my passion to deeply research and write about a topic as complex and fascinating as narratives. Special thanks to Martin Böhringer, David Burnand, Lara Dobson, Juliane Kiesenbauer, Sven Lindenhahn, and Sebastian Hoff for not only helping me create the free time for this project but also being inspirational conversation partners. Thanks to Friedrich Bremer for supporting the entire research and editing phase, especially the extensive research on global master narratives. I am very grateful for the feedback and support from the core editing team: Robert Grover, Lindsey Sullivan, and Gabriella Williams, as well as the many helpful comments and ideas from Ahmed Ali, Lottie Bazley, Emma Fischer, Stephanie Flügel, Carolin Friedemann, Tara Jaf, Leigh Nofi, Charlotte Otter, Roberto Riehle, Stefanie Stotz, and Brian Tomlinson.

Janet Levrel and Alyson von Massow did a fantastic job with the cover design and overall layout of the book. The illustrations at the beginning of each chapter were created with the help of OpenAI's image generator, DALL-E.

I am very thankful for the support of my family and the many friends and colleagues who kept asking, "When is the book going to launch?" That said, perhaps most impactful of all have been the hundreds of Staffbase clients who have inspired us to look beyond the messages and stories that have traditionally received most of the spotlight and turn our attention instead to the audience and the impact that great communication can deliver.

GLOSSARY

Agenda-setting theory suggests that public opinion can be shaped due to what issues are given the most attention.

Alternative narratives provide a different perspective or interpretation of events or ideas than the dominant narrative without directly confronting it.

Biographical master narratives focus on how life should unfold and what a good life looks like.

Counternarratives are narratives created to directly resist or challenge the dominant narrative.

Emerging narratives revolve around new or recent events and are well known to a broad, sometimes global, audience.

Episodic master narratives are specific narratives about past events that are told with great frequency and in relatively the same manner.

Framing is how stories can be connected with narratives, framing references the way in which we present information to influence others' perceptions; also known as second-level agenda-setting.

Local identity is created through deeply embedded narratives for individuals or groups.

Local narratives are a group or individual narratives that are localized by factors such as geographic dimensions, professions, special interests, or social groups.

Master narratives are narratives that have become deeply embedded in the collective mind of a group.

Moat is a term that when used in a business context represents the competitive advantage of a company that is difficult for competitors to imitate or overcome.

Narrative battles are a strategic tug-of-war between competing entities that are aiming to shape public perception in their favor.

Narrative constellations are a collection of narratives which support and amplify each other.

Narrative map is a tool for mapping stories and narratives related to a specific topic or a particular audience.

Narrative moat is a term for the narratives which form an organization's reputation and represent their unique and competitive advantage.

Narrative is the connecting thread of multiple stories that leads to a broader understanding or conclusion.

North Star narrative is a clear and inspirational narrative that focuses on an envisioned future of an organization.

Structural master narratives focus on how stories should be sequenced and played out.

Theory of change (TOC) is a methodology for mapping out a communications strategy; the framework outlines how and why a desired social change is expected to occur through specific intervention.

NOTES

FOREWORD

1. Walker, Thomas G.; Main, Eleanor C. (1973). *Choice Shifts and Extreme Behavior: Judicial Review in the Federal Courts.* The Journal of Social Psychology. 2. 91 (2): pp. 215–221.
2. Lim, S., Bentley, P.J. (2022). *Opinion Amplification Causes Extreme Polarization in Social Networks.* Sci Rep 12, 18131.
3. Bogers, T., & Björneborn, L. (2013). *Micro-serendipity: Meaningful Coincidences in Everyday Life Shared on Twitter.* I Proceedings of the iConference 2013, pp. 196-208.
4. *Two Americas Index: No Politics at Thanksgiving, Please.* (2022). Available at: https://www.axios.com/2022/11/24/thanksgiving-family-politics-midterms-republicans-democrats (Accessed: 19 February 2024).
5. Frimer JA, Skitka LJ. (2020) *Are Politically Diverse Thanksgiving Dinners Shorter Than Politically Uniform Ones?* PLoS One.
6. *2023 Edelman Trust Barometer Global Report* (2023) Edelman. Available at: https://www.edelman.com/sites/g/files/aatuss191/files/2023-03/2023%20Edelman%20Trust%20Barometer%20Global%20Report%20FINAL.pdf (Accessed: 19 December 2023).
7. Global Future Commission. (2022). *Earth for All: A Survival Guide for Humanity.* Global Future Press, p.136.

CHAPTER 1

1. Choe, S. and Sweet, K. (2023) *Bank Runs Used to Be Slow. The Digital Era Sped Them Up,* AP News. Available at: https://apnews.com/article/silicon-valley-bank-bank-run-twitter-fdic-fdbfc08ed00fcbdb9d83897b1b9f42ae (Accessed: 15 November 2023).
2. Sam Altman (@sama) (2023) [Twitter] 12 March. Available at: https://twitter.com/sama/status/1634958188759101441?lang=de (Accessed: 15 November 2023).

3. Harari, Y.N. (2022) in *Sapiens: A Brief History of Humankind.* Toronto, Ontario: Signal, McClelland & Stewart, p. 36.

4. Fombrun, C.J. (1996) in *Reputation: Realizing Value from the Corporate Image.* Boston: Harvard Business School Press, p. 61.

5. *Best Global Brands - The 100 Most Valuable Global Brands* (2023) Interbrand. Available at: https://interbrand.com/best-brands/ (Accessed: 19 December 2023).

6. Aula, P. and Mantere, S. (2008) *Strategic Reputation Management: Towards a Company of Good.* New York: Routledge.

7. Ibid.

8. Ross, T. (2023) *Building Reputation in 2023: The Link Between Corporate Reputation and Business Efficiency*, IPSOS. Available at: https://www.ipsos.com/en/building-reputation-2023-link-between-corporate-reputation-and-business-efficiency (Accessed: 19 December 2023).

9. Cook, F., & Farrell, S. (2023). *2023 Global Communication Report.* USC Annenberg Center for Public Relations.

10. Loizos, C. (2023) *Silicon Valley Bank Shoots Self in Foot,* TechCrunch. Available at: https://techcrunch.com/2023/03/09/silicon-valley-bank-shoots-self-in-foot/ (Accessed: 15 November 2023).

11. Fairhurst, G.T. (2021) in *The Power of Framing: Creating the Language of Leadership.* San Francisco: Jossey-Bass, A Wiley Brand, p. 22.

12. Lulu Cheng Meservey (@lulumeservey) (2023) [Twitter] 10 March. Available at: https://twitter.com/lulumeservey/status/1634232322693144576 (Accessed: 15 November 2023).

13. Schroeder, P. and Lang, H. (2023) *Us Regulator Cites "Terrible" Risk Management for Silicon Valley Bank Failure,* Reuters. Available at: https://www.reuters.com/markets/us/us-regulators-face-sharp-questions-congress-over-bank-collapses-2023-03-28/ (Accessed: 19 December 2023).

14. Fombrun, C.J. (1996) in *Reputation: Realizing Value from the Corporate Image.* Boston: Harvard Business School Press, p. 52.

15. Thorbecke, C. (2023) *Google Shares Lose $100 Billion After Company's Ai Chatbot Makes an Error During Demo,* CNN. Available at: https://edition.cnn.com/2023/02/08/tech/google-ai-bard-demo-error/index.html (Accessed: 19 December 2023).

16. Friedman, M. (1970) *A Friedman Doctrine — The Social Responsibility of Business Is to Increase Its Profits,* The New York Times. Available at: https://www.nytimes.com/1970/09/13/archives/a-friedman-doctrine-the-social-responsibility-of-business-is-to.html (Accessed: 15 November 2023).

17. Our Commitment (no date) *Business Roundtable — Opportunity*. Available at: https://opportunity.businessroundtable.org/ourcommitment/ (Accessed: 15 November 2023).

18. *Billionaire No More: Patagonia Founder Gives Away the Company*, The New York Times. Available at: https://www.nytimes.com/2022/09/14/climate/patagonia-climate-philanthropy-chouinard.html (Accessed: 26 February 2024).

19. *The Future of Corporate Communications* (2023) Edelman. Available at: https://www.edelman.com/sites/g/files/aatuss191/files/2023-09/Executive%20Summary%20-%202023%20Edelman%20Future%20of%20Corporate%20Communications%20Study.pdf (Accessed: 19 December 2023).

20. *2023 Edelman Trust Barometer Global Report* (2023) Edelman. Available at: https://www.edelman.com/sites/g/files/aatuss191/files/2023-03/2023%20Edelman%20Trust%20Barometer%20Global%20Report%20FINAL.pdf (Accessed: 19 December 2023).

21. Castrodale, J. (2021) *Ronaldo Chooses Water Over Coca-Cola, Causing Soda Shares to Drop*, Food & Wine. Available at: https://www.foodandwine.com/news/christiano-ronaldo-coke-water-comment-european-cup (Accessed: 19 December 2023).

22. *WFA Launches the State of Advertising Report* (2019) WFA. Available at: https://wfanet.org/knowledge/item/2019/06/18/WFA-launches-The-State-of-Advertising-report (Accessed: 19 December 2023).

23. Weimann, J. (2023) in *Einfach zu einfach: Wie die leichten Lösungen unsere Demokratie bedrohen*. S.l.: Springer, pp. 142–143.

24. Vosoughi, S., Roy, D. and Aral, S. (2018) *The Spread of True and False News Online*, Science, 359(6380), pp. 1146–1151. doi:10.1126/science.aap9559.

25. Hess, G. (2018) *Surprisingly, Authentic Less-produced Videos Get Better Engagement*, LinkedIn. Available at: https://www.linkedin.com/pulse/make-bad-videos-get-better-engagement-garin-hess/ (Accessed: 19 December 2023).

26. Bradley, D. (2023) *A Stanley Cup Survived a Car Fire and Went Viral. Then the Brand Gave the Owner a New Vehicle*, PR Week. Available at: https://www.prweek.com/article/1848220/stanley-cup-survived-car-fire-went-viral-brand-gave-owner-new-vehicle (Accessed: 19 December 2023).

27. Mike McGuiness (@mikemcg0) (2023) [Twitter] 6 October. Available at: https://twitter.com/mikemcg0/status/1710283791674048550 (Accessed: 15 November 2023).

28. *2023 Edelman Trust Barometer Global Report* (2023) Edelman. Available at: https://www.edelman.com/sites/g/files/aatuss191/files/2023-03/2023%20Edelman%20Trust%20Barometer%20Global%20Report%20FINAL.pdf (Accessed: 19 December 2023).

29. *The Future of Corporate Communications* (2023) Edelman. Available at: https://www.edelman.com/sites/g/files/aatuss191/files/2023-09/Executive%20Summary%20-%202023%20Edelman%20Future%20of%20Corporate%20Communications%20Study.pdf (Accessed: 19 December 2023).

30. *Environmental, Social and Governance Report 2022 - Silicon Valley Bank* (2022) SVB. Available at: https://www.svb.com/globalassets/library/uploadedfiles/svb_environmental_social_governance_report_2022.pdf (Accessed: 19 December 2023).

31. Schroeder, P. and Lang, H. (2023) *US Regulator Cites "Terrible" Risk Management for Silicon Valley Bank Failure*, Reuters. Available at: https://www.reuters.com/markets/

us/us-regulators-face-sharp-questions-congress-over-bank-collapses-2023-03-28/ (Accessed: 19 December 2023).

32. Howard Lerman (@howard) (2023) [Twitter] 9 March. Available at: https://twitter.com/howard/status/1633908101534367746?cxt=HHwWhIC2ud6w56wtAAAA (Accessed: 15 November 2023).
33. Doorley, J. and Garcia, H.F. (2021) in *Reputation Management: The Key to Successful Public Relations and Corporate Communication.* New York: Routledge, Taylor & Francis Group.
34. (2017) *TOWARD NEW GRAVITY Charting a Course for the Narrative Initiative.* rep. Narrative Initiative. Available at: https://narrativeinitiative.org/resource/toward-new-gravity/ (Accessed: 13 November 2023).
35. *Google* (2023) *Wikipedia.* Available at: https://en.wikipedia.org/wiki/Google (Accessed: 19 December 2023).
36. *Google Code of Conduct* (no date) Alphabet Investor Relations. Available at: https://abc.xyz/investor/google-code-of-conduct/ (Accessed: 19 December 2023).
37. Fombrun, C.J., Gardberg, N.A. and Sever, J.M. (2000) *The Reputation Quotient: A Multi-Stakeholder Measure of Corporate Reputation*, The Journal of Brand Management, 7(4), pp. 241–255. doi:10.1057/bm.2000.10.
38. Evan Carmichael (2022) *The Greatest Are Self-Managing | Steve Jobs | #Shorts.* Available at: https://www.youtube.com/watch?v=kd0Og5KlPzY (Accessed: 19 December 2023).
39. Vaswani, A. et al. (2017) *Attention Is All You Need,* NEURIPS. Available at: https://proceedings.neurips.cc/paper_files/paper/2017/file/3f5ee243547dee91fbd053c1c4a845aa-Paper.pdf (Accessed: 19 December 2023).
40. Weimann, J. (2023) in *Einfach zu einfach: Wie die leichten Lösungen unsere Demokratie bedrohen.* S.l.: Springer, p. 93. Author's translation.
41. Ibid., p. 157.
42. Brooks, P. (2022) in *Seduced by Story: The Use and Abuse of Narrative.* New York: New York Review Books, p. 15.

CHAPTER 2

1. Farrell, J. and Goldsmith, P. (2017) in *How to Lose a Referendum: The Definitive Story of Why the UK Voted for Brexit.* London: Biteback Publishing, p. 536.
2. David Beckham (@davidbeckham) (2016) [Instagram]. 21 June Available at: https://www.instagram.com/p/BG6GT7fTWY3/?utm_source=ig_embed&ig_rid=4a944a81-d01b-4273-af31-d357ecffe8d7 (Accessed: 13 November 2023).
3. *EU Referendum: What's on the Minds of Voters?* (2016) The Guardian. Available at: https://www.theguardian.com/politics/2016/jun/15/eu-referendum-whats-on-the-minds-of-voters (Accessed: 13 November 2023).

4. Farrell, J. and Goldsmith, P. (2017) in *How to Lose a Referendum: The Definitive Story of Why the UK Voted for Brexit.* London: Biteback Publishing, p. 564.
5. Pinker, S. (2009) in *How the Mind Works.* New York (N.Y.): W.W. Norton, p. 543.
6. Zak, P.J. (2015) *Why Inspiring Stories Make Us React: The Neuroscience of Narrative,* Cerebrum. Available at: https://www.ncbi.nlm.nih.gov/pmc/articles/PMC4445577/ (Accessed: 13 November 2023).
7. Sabater, V. (2022) *How Mental Narratives Are Formed in the Brain,* Exploring Your Mind. Available at: https://exploringyourmind.com/how-mental-narratives-are-formed-in-the-brain/ (Accessed: 13 November 2023).
8. Bruner, J.S. (1990) *Acts of Meaning: Four Lectures on Mind and Culture.* Cambridge, MA: Harvard University Press.
9. Cohn-Sheehy, B.I. et al. (2021) *The Hippocampus Constructs Narrative Memories Across Distant Events,* Current Biology, 31(22). doi:10.1016/j.cub.2021.09.013.
10. Entman, Robert (1993) *Framing: Towards a Clarification of a Fractured Paradigm.* Journal of Communication 43 (3), p. 51–58.
11. BBC News (2016) *Michael Gove on David Beckham's Decision to "Remain" in the EU,* BBC News. Available at: https://www.youtube.com/watch?v=gp8xpXVi2IE (Accessed: 13 November 2023).
12. Bruner, J. (1986). *Actual Minds, Possible Worlds.* Cambridge, MA: Harvard University Press. p. 13.
13. Akerlof, G., and D.J. Snower (2016), *Bread and Bullets,* Journal of Economic Behavior and Organization, 126, pp. 58–71.
14. Corman, S.R. (2013) *The Difference between Story and Narrative,* CSC Center for Strategic Communication. Available at: https://csc.asu.edu/2013/03/21/the-difference-between-story-and-narrative/ (Accessed: 13 November 2023).
15. Erlach, C. and Müller, M. (2020) in *Narrative Organisationen: Wie die Arbeit mit Geschichten Unternehmen zukunftsfähig macht.* Springer Gabler, p. 126.
16. *The Features of Narratives: A Model of Narrative Form for Social Change Efforts* (2021) FrameWorks Institute. Available at: https://www.frameworksinstitute.org/publication/the-features-of-narratives-a-model-of-narrative-form-for-social-change-efforts/ (Accessed: 15 November 2023).
17. Erlach, C. and Müller, M. (2020) in *Narrative Organisationen: Wie die Arbeit mit Geschichten Unternehmen zukunftsfähig macht.* Springer Gabler, p. 150.
18. Farrell, J. and Goldsmith, P. (2017) in *How to Lose a Referendum: The Definitive Story of Why the UK Voted for Brexi.* London: Biteback Publishing, p. 442.

CHAPTER 3

1. Palmer Luckey, (2022) *All-In Summit: Palmer Luckey on Anduril*, Available at: https://www.youtube.com/watch?v=nK0NfL2M5L4
2. *Tech's Most Controversial Startup Now Makes Drone-Killing Robots* (2019) Bloomberg. Available at: https://www.bloomberg.com/news/features/2019-10-03/tech-s-most-controversial-startup-now-makes-attack-drones (Accessed: 27 December 2023).
3. *"The Business of War": Google Employees Protest Work for the Pentagon* (2018) New York Times. Available at: https://www.nytimes.com/2018/04/04/technology/google-letter-ceo-pentagon-project.html (Accessed: 27 December 2023).
4. *The End of History and the Last Man* (2023) Wikipedia. Available at: https://en.wikipedia.org/wiki/The_End_of_History_and_the_Last_Man (Accessed: 27 December 2023).
5. Borsari, Federico & Davis Jr., Gordon B. (2023). *Drones Are Changing Warfare — The EU Needs to Catch Up*. Politico. Available at: https://www.politico.eu/article/drones-are-changing-warfare-the-eu-needs-to-catch-up-ukraine-gaza-conflicts/. (Accessed: 27 December 2023).
6. *World's Largest Drone Maker Is Unfazed — Even If It's Blacklisted by the U.S.* (2023) CNBC. Available at: https://www.cnbc.com/2023/02/08/worlds-largest-drone-maker-dji-is-unfazed-by-challenges-like-us-blacklist.html (Accessed: 27 December 2023).
7. *Silicon Valley Goes to War* (2023) TechCrunch. Available at: https://techcrunch.com/2023/02/15/defense-tech-startups-war/ (Accessed: 27 December 2023).
8. Benedict, C., Sanjeev, G. and Saida, K. (2021) *Military Spending in the Post-Pandemic Era,* IMF F&D, IMF. Available at: https://www.imf.org/external/pubs/ft/fandd/2021/06/military-spending-in-the-post-pandemic-era-clements-gupta-khamidova.htm (Accessed: 27 December 2023).
9. McLean, K.C. and Syed, M. (2019) *Personal, Master, and Alternative Narratives: An Integrative Framework for Understanding Identity Development in Context* [Preprint]. doi:10.31234/osf.io/s6vtq. p. 15
10. Jeffrey Danese (2022) *This Is Water,* David Foster Wallace Commencement Speech. Available at: https://www.youtube.com/watch?v=DCbGM4mqEVw (Accessed: 15 November 2023).
11. *Geert Hofstede* (2023) Wikipedia. Available at: https://en.wikipedia.org/wiki/Geert_Hofstede (Accessed: 15 November 2023).
12. *Country Comparison Tool* (no date) Hofstede Insights. Available at: https://www.hofstede-insights.com/country-comparison-tool?countries=germany%2Cjapan%2Cunited%2Bstates (Accessed: 15 November 2023).
13. Farrell, J. and Goldsmith, P. (2017) in *How to Lose a Referendum: The Definitive Story of Why the UK Voted for Brexit.* London: Biteback Publishing, p. 601.

14. Shiller, R.J. (2019) in *Narrative Economics: How Stories Go Viral & Drive Major Economic Events.* Princeton; Oxford: Princeton University Press, p. 191.

15. McLean, K.C. and Syed, M. (2019) *Personal, Master, and Alternative Narratives: An Integrative Framework for Understanding Identity Development in Context* [Preprint]. doi:10.31234/osf.io/s6vtq. p. 22.

16. *About Us* (no date) Narrative Initiative. Available at: https://narrativeinitiative.org/about-us/ (Accessed: 15 November 2023).

17. McLean, K.C. and Syed, M. (2019) *Personal, Master, and Alternative Narratives: An Integrative Framework for Understanding Identity Development in Context* [Preprint]. doi:10.31234/osf.io/s6vtq. p. 6.

18. Karlinsky, N. and Stead, J. (2018) *How a Door Became a Desk, And A Symbol of Amazon,* About Amazon.eu. Available at: https://www.aboutamazon.eu/news/working-at-amazon/how-a-door-became-a-desk-and-a-symbol-of-amazon (Accessed: 15 November 2023).

19. Erlach, C., and Müller, M. *Narrative Organisationen.* Berlin/Heidelberg: Springer, p. 352 (Kindle edition). Author's translation.

20. Fischer Appelt, Bernhard. (2022) *Storyverse Playbook: Finde die Geschichten, die alles verändern.* Murmann Verlag.

21. Gad Saad (2023). Twitter. Available at: https://twitter.com/GadSaad/status/1716893409380651407 (Accessed: 15 November 2023).

CHAPTER 4

1. Franck, T. (2019) *Alternative Meat to Become $140 Billion Industry in a Decade, Barclays Predicts,* CNBC. Available at: https://www.cnbc.com/2019/05/23/alternative-meat-to-become-140-billion-industry-barclays-says.html (Accessed: 16 November 2023).

2. Smithers, R. (2018) *"Bleeding" Vegan Burger Arrives on UK Supermarket Shelves,* The Guardian. Available at: https://www.theguardian.com/food/2018/nov/12/bleeding-vegan-burger-arrives-on-uk-supermarket-shelves (Accessed: 16 November 2023).

3. Wilde, W. (2022) *Fact Check: How Bad Is Eating Meat For the Climate?* , dw.com. Available at: https://www.dw.com/en/fact-check-is-eating-meat-bad-for-the-environment (Accessed: 16 November 2023).

4. Reynolds, M. (2023) *Fake Meat Is Bleeding, but It's Not Dead Yet,* WIRED UK. Available at: https://www.wired.co.uk/article/beyond-plant-based-meat (Accessed: 16 November 2023).

5. *Beyond Meat (BYND) Q2 2023 Earnings Call Transcript* (2023) The Motley Fool. Available at: https://www.fool.com/earnings/call-transcripts/2023/08/07/beyond-meat-bynd-q2-2023-earnings-call-transcript/ (Accessed: 16 November 2023).

6. Phoenix, S. (2023) *Vegetarian Statistics 2023: Surprising Facts & Data,* Great Green Wall. Available at: https://www.greatgreenwall.org/supplements/vegetarian-statistics/#:~:text=Over%201.5%20Billion%20people%20worldwide,vegetarian%20because%20of%20economic%20reasons (Accessed: 16 November 2023).
7. *Leon Festinger* (no date) Wikipedia. Available at: https://en.wikipedia.org/wiki/Leon_Festinger (Accessed: 16 November 2023).
8. Halverson, J.R., Goodall, H.L. and Corman, S.R. (2011) *Master Narratives of Islamist Extremism.* New York: Palgrave McMillan, p. 195.
9. Atran, Scott, and Robert Axelrod. *Reframing Sacred Values.* Negotiation Journal, vol. 24, no. 3, July 2008, pp. 221-246.
10. *Brand Re-positioning: Lidl* (2013) slideshare. Available at: https://de.slideshare.net/dixonl3/brand-repositioning-lidl (Accessed: 16 November 2023).
11. Barclay, J. (no date) *Brand Voice Breakdown: Lidl,* The Brand Voice Guy. Available at: https://thebrandvoiceguy.co.uk/lidl-brand-voice/ (Accessed: 16 November 2023).
12. Bedford, E. (2023) *Market Share of Grocery Stores in Great Britain from January 2017 to October 2023,* Statista. Available at: https://www.statista.com/statistics/280208/grocery-market-share-in-the-united-kingdom-uk/ (Accessed: 16 November 2023).
13. Carthy, S. (2021) *Lessons Learned from Alternative Narrative Campaigns,* Radicalisation Awareness Network. Available at: https://home-affairs.ec.europa.eu/system/files/2022-03/ran_lessons_learned_from_alternative_narrative_campaigns_032022_en_1.pdf (Accessed: 16 November 2023).
14. Carthy, S.L. and Sarma, K.M. (2021) *Countering Terrorist Narratives: Assessing the Efficacy and Mechanisms of Change in Counter-narrative Strategies,* Terrorism and Political Violence, 35(3), pp. 569–593. doi:10.1080/09546553.2021.1962308.
15. Quirke, B. (2017) *Making the Connections: Using Internal Communication to Turn Strategy into Action.* Routledge, p. 328.
16. Voss, C. and Raz, T. (2016) *Never Split the Difference: Negotiating As If Your Life Depended on It.* HarperCollins, p. 36.
17. *Empathizing with the Opposition May Make You More Politically Persuasive* (2022) ScienceDaily. Available at: https://www.sciencedaily.com/releases/2022/10/221005132939.htm (Accessed: 16 November 2023).
18. *Australia Day Debate* (no date) Wikipedia. Available at: https://en.wikipedia.org/wiki/Australia_Day_debate (Accessed: 16 November 2023).
19. (2021) Words To Win By [podcast], *Changing the Narrative About First Nations - Australia.* Available at: https://open.spotify.com/episode/2fAAsOCW5j1qRSjwlrmBU1?si=c825863efa1b4521&nd=1
20. Shenker-Osorio, A. (no date) *Messaging This Moment: A Handbook for Progressive Communicators,* Center for Community Change. Available at: https://

communitychange.org/messaging-moment-handbook-progressive-communicators/ (Accessed: 16 November 2023).

21. Schulz, B. (2018) *15 Jahre „Arm, aber sexy"-Spruch: Und heute? Reich, aber öde!*, taz.de. Available at: https://taz.de/15-Jahre-Arm-aber-sexy-Spruch/!5546816/ (Accessed: 16 November 2023).
22. Roxborough, S. (2011) *How Berlin Became the Coolest City on the Planet,* The Hollywood Reporter. Available at: https://www.hollywoodreporter.com/movies/movie-news/berlin-became-coolest-city-planet-97748/ (Accessed: 16 November 2023).
23. Godin, S. (2005) *All Marketers Are Liars.* London: Portfolio Penguin, p. 13.
24. *Causal Layered Analysis* (no date) Wikipedia. Available at: https://en.wikipedia.org/wiki/Causal_layered_analysis (Accessed: 16 November 2023).
25. Inayatullah, S. and Milojević, I. (2015) *CLA 2.0: Transformative Research in Theory and Practice.* Tamsui, Taipei: Tamkang University Press.
26. Grünwald, Dr. Christian et. al. (2021) *Narrative einer erfolgreichen Transformation zu einem ressourcenschonenden und treibhausgasneutralen Deutschland: Erster Zwischenbericht.* Umweltbundesamt. Available at: https://www.umweltbundesamt.de/sites/default/files/medien/5750/publikationen/2021-02-19_texte_26-2021_narrative-rtd2050.pdf (Accessed: 16 November 2023).

CHAPTER 5

1. Isaacson, W. (2023) *Elon Musk.* New York: Simon & Schuster, pp. 91–92.
2. Ibid, p. 100.
3. Borup, M. et al. (2006) *The Sociology of Expectations in Science and Technology*, Technology Analysis & Strategic Management, 18(3–4), pp. 285–298. doi:10.1080/09537320600777002.
4. Senge, P.M. (2009) *The Fifth Discipline: The Art and Practice of the Learning Organisation.* New York: Currency Doubleday, p. 192.
5. *Making Humanity Multiplanetary* (no date) SpaceX. Available at: https://www.spacex.com/mission/ (Accessed: 15 November 2023).
6. *About Blue Origin* (no date) Blue Origin. Available at: https://www.blueorigin.com/about-blue (Accessed: 29 December 2023).
7. Hall, K. (2023) *Stories That Stick: How Storytelling Can Captivate Customers, Influence Audiences, and Transform Your Business.* Nashville, TN: HarperCollins Leadership, p. 48.
8. Barkowski, C. (2022) *How Much It Costs to Fly to Space on Jeff Bezos' Blue Origin Spacecraft,* Running with Miles. Available at: https://runningwithmiles.boardingarea.com/how-much-it-costs-to-fly-to-space-on-jeff-bezos-blue-origin-spacecraft/ (Accessed: 15 November 2023).

9. *Starlink* (no date) Wikipedia. Available at: https://en.wikipedia.org/wiki/Starlink (Accessed: 15 November 2023).

10. O'Shea, C.A. (2023) *NASA Selects Blue Origin as Second Artemis Lunar Lander Provider,* NASA. Available at: https://www.nasa.gov/news-release/nasa-selects-blue-origin-as-second-artemis-lunar-lander-provider/ (Accessed: 15 November 2023).

11. Millionaire Motivation98 (2021) *You Can't Skip Steps. You Have to Put One Foot in Front of the Other.* Available at: https://www.youtube.com/watch?v=-EJ08AKdapQ (Accessed: 15 November 2023).

12. SpaceX (2017) *How Not to Land an Orbital Rocket Booster.* Available at: https://www.youtube.com/watch?v=bvim4rsNHkQ (Accessed: 15 November 2023).

13. FOX Business Staff (2021) *SpaceX Has "Tremendous Lead" Over Blue Origin, Top Physicist Says, Fox Business.* Available at: https://www.foxbusiness.com/technology/michio-kaku-spacex-tremendous-lead-over-blue-origin (Accessed: 15 November 2023).

14. Jones, J.M. (2021) *Americans Revert to Favoring Reduced Government Role,* Gallup News. Available at: https://news.gallup.com/poll/355838/americans-revert-favoring-reduced-government-role.aspx (Accessed: 15 November 2023).

15. *The "Explorer" Gene — Is Adventure In Your Blood?* (2017) Bushgear. Available at: https://www.bushgear.co.uk/blogs/bush-telegraph-2017/the-explorer-gene-is-adventure-in-your-blood (Accessed: 15 November 2023).

16. Isaacson, W. (2023) *Elon Musk.* New York: Simon & Schuster, p. 94.

17. *Blue Origin NS-23* (no date) Wikipedia. Available at: https://en.wikipedia.org/wiki/Blue_Origin_NS-23 (Accessed: 15 November 2023).

18. Isaacson, W. (2023) *Elon Musk.* New York: Simon & Schuster, p. 94.

19. Fauzia, M. (2021) *Fact Check: Jeff Bezos' New Shepard Rocket Launch Didn't Emit Carbon,* USA Today. Available at: https://eu.usatoday.com/story/news/factcheck/2021/07/28/fact-check-jeff-bezos-new-shepard-rocket-launch-didnt-emit-carbon/8073047002/ (Accessed: 15 November 2023).

20. Moskowitz, C. (2022) *Billionaire Space Tourism Has Become Insufferable,* Scientific American. Available at: https://www.scientificamerican.com/article/billionaire-space-tourism-has-become-insufferable/ (Accessed: 15 November 2023).

21. *Our Impact* (no date) Alzheimer's Disease and Dementia. Available at: https://www.alz.org/about/our-impact (Accessed: 15 November 2023).

22. Sull, D., Sull, C. and Yoder, J. (2018) *No One Knows Your Strategy — Not Even Your Top Leaders,* MIT Sloan Management Review. Available at: https://sloanreview.mit.edu/article/no-one-knows-your-strategy-not-even-your-top-leaders/ (Accessed: 15 November 2023).

23. Peiper, H. (2023) *A New Mission for Starbucks,* Starbucks Stories & News. Available at: https://stories.starbucks.com/stories/2023/a-new-mission-for-starbucks/ (Accessed: 15 November 2023).

24. Miskimmon, A., O'Loughlin, B. and Roselle, L. (2014) *Strategic Narratives: Communication Power and the New World Order.* New York: Routledge, Taylor & Francis Group, p. 15.

25. Raskin, A. (2021) The Jam Sessions by Rock Content [podcast], *#9. Story Is Strategy: Strategic Narrative as Your Company's North Star with Andy Raskin.* Available at: https://open.spotify.com/episode/5cVlzHMyhDjgivuZRxOqds?si=3f466f6affe2402c&nd=1

26. *ADI- Dementia Statistics* (no date) Alzheimer's Disease International (ADI). Available at: https://www.alzint.org/about/dementia-facts-figures/dementia-statistics/ (Accessed: 15 November 2023).

27. Shiller, R.J. (2019) in *Narrative Economics: How Stories Go Viral & Drive Major Economic Events.* Princeton/Oxford: Princeton University Press, pp. 65–66.

CHAPTER 6

1. *De Beers' Diamond History - Our Story: De Beers UK* (no date) *De Beers UK.* Available at: https://www.debeers.co.uk/en-gb/our-story.html (Accessed: 15 November 2023).

2. Epstein, E.J. (1982) *Have You Ever Tried to Sell a Diamond?,* The Atlantic. Available at: https://www.theatlantic.com/magazine/archive/1982/02/have-you-ever-tried-to-sell-a-diamond/304575/?single_page=true (Accessed: 15 November 2023).

3. Kolowich Cox, L. (2014) *The Engagement Ring Story: How De Beers Created a Multi-Billion Dollar Industry From the Ground Up, HubSpot Blog.* Available at: https://blog.hubspot.com/marketing/diamond-de-beers-marketing-campaign (Accessed: 15 November 2023).

4. Garside, M. (2023) *Diamond Industry - Statistics & Facts,* Statista. Available at: https://www.statista.com/topics/1704/diamond-industry/#topicOverview (Accessed: 15 November 2023).

5. *Diamond Market Size, Share, Industry Forecast by 2032* (no date) Emergen Research. Available at: https://www.emergenresearch.com/industry-report/diamond-market#:~:-text=The%20global%20diamond%20market%20size,3.0%25%20during%20the%20forecast%20period (Accessed: 15 November 2023).

6. Harden, B. (2000) *Diamond Wars: A special report.; Africa's Gems: Warfare's Best Friend.* New York Times. Available at: https://www.nytimes.com/2000/04/06/world/diamond-wars-a-special-report-africa-s-gems-warfare-s-best-friend.html (Accessed: 24 May 2024).

7. Thompson, Sophie (2022) *Top Leatherworker Reveals What It Really Costs for Louis Vuitton to Make a £1500 Bag,* indy100. Available at: https://www.indy100.com/lifestyle/louis-vuitton-bag-factory-cost (Accessed: 27 March 2024).

8. Rupp, M. (2019) *Vom Shitstorm zur Love Brand – Dr. Martell Beck von der BVG,* Mashup Communications. Available at: https://www.mashup-communications.de/2019/08/podcast-brand-storytelling-martell-beck-bvg/ (Accessed: 15 November 2023).

9. Spannagel, L. (2018) *Warum sind die Berliner, wie sie sind? Berlin verändert das Gehirn*, Tagesspiegel. Available at: https://www.tagesspiegel.de/berlin/berlin-verandert-das-gehirn-5923717.html (Accessed: 15 November 2023).

10. Bersin, Josh (2022) *Recruiting Is Harder Than It Looks: 74% Of Companies Underperform*, Available at: https://joshbersin.com/2022/04/reccruiting-is-harder-than-it-looks-74-of-companies-underperform/ (Accessed: 04 January 2024).

11. Blaine Allen (@BlainLikeBrain) (2023) [Twitter] 18 September. Available at: https://twitter.com/BlaineLikeBrain/status/1703834902934782258?s=20 (Accessed: 15 November 2023).

12. Adams, Bryan; Marshall, Charlotte. (2020) *Give & Get Employer Branding: Repel the Many and Compel the Few with Impact, Purpose and Belonging*. Houndstooth Press, p.77.

13. Ibid, p. 28

14. Arnold, Sarah (2019) *Of Course McDonald's Paper Straws Can't Be Recycled – It's Yet Another Corporate Green Wash*, Independent. Available at: https://www.independent.co.uk/voices/mcdonalds-plastic-straws-recycling-carbon-footprint-green-washing-waste-starbucks-a9041871.html (Accessed: 04 January 2024).

15. *Packaging, Toys & Waste*, McDonald's, https://corporate.mcdonalds.com/corpmcd/our-purpose-and-impact/our-planet/packaging-toys-and-waste.html (Accessed: 10 May 2024).

16. Doorley, John; Garcia, Helio Fred. *Reputation Management* (2021). Taylor and Francis, p. 8.

17. Risen, J. (1988) *"I've Taken a Beating": Lee Iacocca Falls From Public Grace*, Los Angeles Times. Available at: https://www.latimes.com/archives/la-xpm-1988-05-03-mn-2137-story.html (Accessed: 15 November 2023).

18. Lovelace, J.B. et al. (2018) *The Shackles of CEO Celebrity: Sociocognitive and Behavioral Role Constraints on "Star" Leaders*, Academy of Management Review, 43(3), pp. 419–444. doi:10.5465/amr.2016.0064.

19. Dewar, C., Hirt, M. and Keller, S. (2019) *The Mindsets and Practices of Excellent CEOs*, McKinsey & Company. Available at: https://www.mckinsey.com/capabilities/strategy-and-corporate-finance/our-insights/the-mindsets-and-practices-of-excellent-ceos (Accessed: 15 November 2023).

20. *Stock Prices Increase When New CEOs Discuss Strategy Publicly, According to New Research* (no date) AESC. Available at: https://www.aesc.org/insights/blog/stock-prices-increase-when-new-ceos-discuss-strategy-publicly-according-new-research (Accessed: 15 November 2023).

21. Witt, S. (2023) *How Jensen Huang's NVIDIA is Powering the A.I. Revolution*, The New Yorker. Available at: https://www.newyorker.com/magazine/2023/12/04/how-jensen-huangs-nvidia-is-powering-the-ai-revolution (Accessed: 29 February 2024).

22. Bass, B.M. (1990) *From transactional to transformational leadership: Learning to share the Vision*, Organizational Dynamics, 18(3), pp. 19–31. doi:10.1016/0090-2616(90)90061-s.

23. Judge, T.A. and Piccolo, R.F. (2004) *Transformational and Transactional Leadership: A Meta-Analytic Test of Their Relative Validity*, Journal of Applied Psychology, 89(5), pp. 755–768. doi:10.1037/0021-9010.89.5.755.

24. Kaufman, M. (no date) *The Carbon Footprint Sham*, Mashable. Available at: https://mashable.com/feature/carbon-footprint-pr-campaign-sham (Accessed: 15 November 2023).

25. Weimann, J. (2023) *Einfach zu einfach: Wie die leichten Lösungen unsere Demokratie bedrohen.* Springer, p. 141.

26. Jankowicz, N. (2020) *How to Lose the Information War: Russia, Fake News, and the Future of Conflict.* London: I.B. Tauris.

27. (2022) *Record Clean Energy Spending Is Set To Help Global Energy Investment Grow by 8% in 2022* [Preprint]. iea. Available at: https://www.iea.org/news/record-clean-energy-spending-is-set-to-help-global-energy-investment-grow-by-8-in-2022.

28. Eccles, R.G., Newquist, S.C. and Schatz, R. (2007) *Reputation and Its Risks*, Harvard Business Review. Available at: https://hbr.org/2007/02/reputation-and-its-risks (Accessed: 15 November 2023).

29. Kolowich Cox, L. (2014) *The Engagement Ring Story: How De Beers Created a Multi-Billion Dollar Industry From the Ground Up*, HubSpot Blog. Available at: https://blog.hubspot.com/marketing/diamond-de-beers-marketing-campaign (Accessed: 15 November 2023).

CHAPTER 7

1. Smith, E. (2023) *The Barbenheimer Phenomenon: What Social Data Tells Us*, Brandwatch. Available at: https://www.brandwatch.com/blog/barbenheimer/ (Accessed: 30 November 2023).

2. Shiller, R.J. (2019) in *Narrative Economics: How Stories Go Viral & Drive Major Economic Events.* Princeton; Oxford: Princeton University Press, p. 68.

3. Rubin, R. (2023) *Inside* "Barbie's" *Pink Publicity Machine: How Warner Bros. Pulled Off the Marketing Campaign of the Year*, Variety. Available at: https://variety.com/2023/film/box-office/barbie-marketing-campaign-explained-warner-bros-1235677922/ (Accessed: 30 November 2023).

4. Berger, M. (2009): *Planungsillusion und Improvisation: Experimente zum Prozessmusterwechsel.* Seminar paper at the Institute for International Management at the Universität der Bundeswehr München. Available at: https://docplayer.org/21884941-Planungsillusion-und-improvisation-experimente-zum-prozessmuster-wechsel-seminararbeit.html (Accessed: 30 November 2023).

5. Cain, S. and Holmes, O. (2023) *Barbenheimer Backlash: Warner Bros Apologises After Its Japan Arm Complains*, The Guardian. Available at: https://www.theguardian.com/

film/2023/aug/01/not-big-in-japan-country-rejects-co-marketing-of-barbie-and-oppenheimer-as-trivialising-nuclear-war (Accessed: 30 November 2023).

6. Martin, R.L. (2022) *A New Way to Think: Your Guide to Superior Management Effectiveness.* Boston, MA: Harvard Business Review Press.

7. Eldersch, T. (2022) *„Der Klimawandel wird so viel dahinraffen" – Bayern braucht mehr Windkraft – und das schnell,* Merkur.de. Available at: https://www.merkur.de/bayern/klimawandel-windkraft-experte-holzheu-soeder-csu-ausbau-artenschutz-bayern-zr-91949597.html (Accessed: 30 November 2023).

8. Personal interview with Carolin Friedemann, founder and Managing Director of Initiative Klimaneutrales Deutschland, conducted on October 26, 2023.

9. Sebald, C. (2023) 432 *Bürgermeister fordern von Söder mehr Tempo bei Windkraftausbau,* Süddeutsche.de. Available at: https://www.sueddeutsche.de/bayern/bayern-energiewende-markus-soeder-buergermeister-appell-1.6112261 (Accessed: 30 November 2023).

10. Dencheva, V. (2023) *Global Influencer Marketing Value 2016-2023,* Statista. Available at: https://www.statista.com/statistics/1092819/global-influencer-market-size/#:~:text=The%20global%20influencer%20marketing%20market,record%2021.1%20billion%20U.S.%20dollars (Accessed: 30 November 2023).

11. Kyle O'Brien (2019) *Ads We Like: Ryan Reynolds' Aviation Gin Enlists Peloton Wife to Down a Gin Martini in a Zinger.* Available at: adhttps://www.thedrum.com/news/2019/12/07/ads-we-ryan-reynolds-aviation-gin-enlists-peloton-wife-down-gin-martini-zinger-ad (Accessed: 30 November 2023).

12. Grunig, J.E. (2006) *Furnishing the edifice: Ongoing research on public relations as a strategic management function,* Journal of Public Relations Research, 18(2), pp. 151–176. doi:10.1207/s1532754xjprr1802_5.

13. Chotia, Y. (2022) *Haier: The Founding Myth o Creative Destruction, Management Made in China.* Available at: https://chinese-management.com/en/haier-the-founding-myth-of-creative-destruction/ (Accessed: 30 November 2023).

14. Nielsen, J. (2023) *AI Improves Employee Productivity by 66%,* Nielsen Norman Group. Available at: https://www.nngroup.com/articles/ai-tools-productivity-gains/ (Accessed: 30 November 2023).

15. Dell'Acqua, F. et al. (2023) *Navigating the jagged technological frontier: Field experimental evidence of the effects of AI on knowledge worker productivity and quality,* SSRN Electronic Journal, 24–013. doi:10.2139/ssrn.4573321.

16. Moore, M. and Sen, R. (2022) *Funding Narrative Change, An Assessment and Framework,* Convergence Partnership. Available at: https://convergencepartnership.org/publication/funding-narrative-change-an-assessment-and-framework/ (Accessed: 30 November 2023).

CHAPTER 8

1. (2023) *Jens Ritter on LinkedIn.* Available at: https://www.linkedin.com/posts/jens-ritter_wetakeofftotakecare-changeperspectives-cabincrew-activity-7098227992987852800-7Aot/ (Accessed: 31 January 2024).
2. Personal interview with Stefanie Stotz, Head of Communications and Cultural Development at Lufthansa Airlines, conducted on October 30, 2023.
3. *Willie Walsh Report on the Air Transport Industry* (2023) IATA. Available at: https://www.iata.org/en/pressroom/2023-speeches/2023-06-05-01/ (Accessed: 31 January 2024).
4. Keuschnigg, M., van de Rijt, A. and Bol, T. (2023) *The Plateauing of Cognitive Ability Among Top Earners*, European Sociological Review, 39(5), pp. 820–833. doi:10.1093/esr/jcac076.
5. Hansen, S. et al. (2021) *The Demand for Executive Skills* [Preprint]. doi:10.3386/w28959.
6. (2023) *Jens Ritter on LinkedIn.* Available at: https://www.linkedin.com/posts/jens-ritter_feedback-wetakeofftotakecare-involveme-activity-7109428639510712320-f6tz/?utm_source=share&utm_medium=member_desktop (Accessed: 31 January 2024).
7. Reeves, M., Love, C. and Tillmanns, P. (no date) *Your Strategy Needs a Strategy,* Harvard Business Review. Available at: https://hbr.org/2012/09/your-strategy-needs-a-strategy (Accessed: 31 January 2024).
8. Coyle, D. (2018) *The Culture Code: The Secrets of Highly Successful Groups.* London: Random House Business Books.
9. (2023) *Jens Ritter on LinkedIn.* Available at: https://www.linkedin.com/posts/jens-ritter_wetakeofftotakecare-culturaldevelopment-psychologicalsafety-activity-7103389710286299136-LeTz (Accessed: 31 January 2024).
10. Nadella, S. et al. (2019) in *Hit Refresh: The Quest to Rediscover Microsoft's Soul and Imagine a Better Future for Everyone.* New York: Harper Business, an imprint of HarperCollins Publishers, pp. 100–101.
11. Ibid, p. 76.
12. *2021 The Future of Corporate Communications* (2021) Edelman. Available at: https://www.edelman.com/expertise/commstech/2021-Future-of-Corporate-Comms-Research (Accessed: 31 January 2024).
13. *The CCO as Pacesetter.* (2019) Available at: https://knowledge.page.org/wp-content/uploads/2019/09/CCO_as_Pacesetter_2019_Page_Research_Executive_Summary.pdf (Accessed: 31 January 2024).

14. Simpson, K. (2023) *Introducing the CCO: Why It's Time To Bring Communications Into the C-Suite*, Hanson Search. Available at: https://www.hansonsearch.com/our-insight/articles/introducing-the-cco-why-its-time-to-bring-communications-into-c-suite/ (Accessed: 31 January 2024).

15. *It's All About Content – Strategic Topic Management in Agile Organizations* (2019) Academic Society. Available at: https://www.akademische-gesellschaft.com/publikation/its-all-about-content/?lang=en (Accessed: 31 January 2024).

16. Mickeleit, T. and Forthmann, J. (2023) in *Erfolgsfaktor Commtech: Die digitale Transformation der Unternehmenskommunikation.* Wiesbaden, Germany: Springer Gabler, p. 46.

17. SparkToro (2023) *Office Hours: The End of Marketing Attribution*, Available at: https://www.youtube.com/watch?v=PGomifZVP1U (Accessed: 31 January 2024).

Made in the USA
Las Vegas, NV
03 January 2025